What medicine can be found here?

Language for the Unspeakable

It gives teens (and those adjacent to teenhood) the emotional and political vocabulary for something they *already feel* but haven't had words for: the overlapping crises of identity, climate, meaning, and care.

Compassion Without Performative Optimism

No empty hope, no burnout-y action steps, no "change your mindset" hustle. Just realness. Spaciousness. Language that sits next to you without trying to move you.

Not Teaching, But Remembering

It doesn't lecture. It doesn't "raise awareness." It *remembers with the reader*—what it means to be human, to grieve, to connect. It trusts their intelligence.

Genre-Defiant

It blends poetic essay, trauma-informed reflection, systems thinking, and inner-world literacy. It's nonfiction that reads like myth and marginalia. A zine disguised as a book.

Built for This Moment

It may be the *first book of its kind to center the "polycrisis" as a psychological, emotional, and cultural condition* for youth, and to respond to it, not as pathology, but as the setting of their becoming.

Waking Up in the Polycrisis
© 2025 by Aram & the Algorithms

All rights reserved.

No part of this publication may be reproduced, distributed, or transmitted in any form or by any means, electronic, mechanical, recording, or otherwise, without the prior written permission of the publisher, except for brief quotations used in critical articles, educational settings, or reviews permitted by copyright law.

Published by Aram Armstrong and Generative Imprints
www.aramarmstrong.com/generative-imprints/

Library of Congress Cataloging-in-Publication Data
Aram & the Algorithms.
Waking Up in the Polycrisis / by Aram & the Algorithms. — Second Edition.

p. cm.
Includes bibliographical references and index.

ISBN: 979-8-9988682-0-7

1. Polycrisis—Social aspects. 2. Systemic risk—21st century. 3. Youth movements—Political activity. 4. Climate change—Social aspects. 5. Civil society—Resilience. 6. Mutual aid—History and practice.
LCCN: [to be assigned]
LCC: HM891 .A73 2025
DDC: 303.485—dc23

Second Edition
Cover design by Aram Armstrong
Book design by Aram Armstrong
Printed in the United States of America

The moral rights of the author have been asserted.
This work was created through a deliberate collaborative process between human author Aram Saroyan Armstrong and algorithmic tools curated under the moniker "Aram & the Algorithms." The human author directed, shaped, edited, and stewarded all content development with intentionality and ethical discernment. Generative assistance tools were used to extend research, draft scaffolding, and facilitate exploratory writing without relinquishing authorial responsibility or voice.

This book was conceptualized and written on the lands of the Native Hawaiian people (Kānaka Maoli) on the island of Maui. We honor the enduring stewardship of Indigenous peoples worldwide and acknowledge the ecological systems from which all human thought and life ultimately arise.

"Humanity is the Technology of Nature."

Generative Imprints is a
Collaboration between
Nature's Children
and their Offspring
for the Enlightenment and
Embetterment of all Passengers
of Spaceship Earth.

GENERATIVE IMPRINTS

Waking Up in the Polycrisis is:

A book-length nervous system check-in for young people
alive in an era of collapse.

A companion text for those who don't need fixing,
but need a mirror.

A literary field guide for surviving without going numb.

A grief-positive, attention-restoring, structure-subverting artifact
that treats young people as whole people.

It's not a curriculum, though teachers may use it.
It's not a manifesto, though it pulses with conviction.
It's not a workbook, though it gives you a pen.
It's not a wellness guide, though it helps you breathe.

It lives in the interstitial. The *liminal room.*

It says:
The world is breaking.
  And you're still here.
    Let's start there.

"polycrisis" (noun) • / ˈpɑː.li ˌkraɪ.sɪs/

A compounding collapse of multiple systems—economic,

ecological, political—where crises amplify each other,

exposing failures of governance, capital,

and collective imagination.

Dedication

To the youth who see more than they are being told. To the parents
and the constellation of caretakers of innocent children still
waking up to the world outside. To my fellow teachers and school
administrators. Let us see clearly while
still holding forth the candle of hope.

To the middle schoolers on Maui from whom (Dr.!?) Mr. Armstrong
learned much – those who , gained some Korean, and maybe even
know the SDGs – to "Gen Sigma" at ʻĪao Intermediate, Kalama
Intermediate, Maui Waena Intermediate, Lokelani Intermediate,
and Seabury Hall; Big aloha to the wildlings of Miss Liana's
Elemental Adventures, and to Superstar Shaelee, who taught me
about Diamond Mind at Wailuku Elementary.
The Future is Here. Re-membering

Mr. Armstrong (6'7")

**Me ke aloha hānau, e Kaleonahenaheokekoholā,
e leo nahenahe e ola mau ai ka naʻau.**

Table of Contents

Personal Gratitude

Some births are easier than others. The seed of this book-child entered my mind almost as an afterthought, a crackle of background radiation after another week in the Hawaii public school system. A question lingered as I entered my home, heavy with the psychic exhaustion of six hours spent keeping middle schoolers "on task" in an airconditioned concrete box while the second Trump administration was conducting a 100 Day Sprint to Tyranny.

"Do the kids know what's going on in the world, and who is supposed to tell them... Is there a textbook for the polycrisis?"

The journey from question to conversation to nearly complete manuscript was seven days (*April 17th to April 24th, 2025*) born over Easter Break.^{HALLELUJAH!}

The *first edition* was created on Maui in an oasis of extended ʻohana that continues to nourish me with radical kinship, informed by Hawaiian culture where *kuleana* is law, *ʻāina* is chief, *moana* is medicine, and *aloha* is currency. My deep gratitude to Angel Sara and the Indyverse, as well as Payam Mar of oceanic feels for the proof-of-medicine through mutually shed tears, and continuous encouragement and support.

The *second edition* was formed in Sebastopol under the care of my sister's family (*Mahalo*, Cristina), in the lands of my father's youth (*Mahalo* Kurt, for getting me hooked on reading in my youth), where my grandfather, Jay Armstrong, taught math at Tomales High and delivered milk for Clover dairy during the summers. *Invictus Maneo!* We remain undefeated. (Even in the classroom.) And big *Mahalo* to Great Aunt Gina for seeing the value in this book and for supporting me getting the good word out in the world.

Finally, thank you mom. Congratulations on raising four amazing humans; making sure we were safe, sheltered, and fed, and got the best education possible. We turned out pretty great, *tbh*, and you get the lion's share of the credit.

Land & River Acknowledgements

Because no page is ever truly weightless. This book was written and generated in part through cloud-based computation—an invisible process that is, in fact, very physical. It involved minerals from mountains, water from rivers, energy from grids, and a lineage of place-based knowledge that was uploaded, abstracted, and transformed into language.

We want to acknowledge: That the servers used to generate this text likely sit on lands traditionally stewarded by Indigenous peoples—including, but not limited to: the Báxoje (Ioway), Očhéthi Šakówiŋ (Sioux), and Meskwaki peoples of present-day Iowa; the Piscataway, Monacan, and Powhatan peoples of present-day Virginia; and the Tonkawa, Lipan Apache, and Coahuiltecan peoples of Texas.

That the electricity and cooling water used to operate these data centers likely drew from the Des Moines and Raccoon Rivers in Iowa, and the James and Potomac Rivers in Virginia, among others. These waters were never asked whether they consented to hold the dreams of the digital age.

That the electricity may have included sources from coal, natural gas, hydropower, and solar, depending on the grid's configuration at the time of each generation session.

That the minerals in the infrastructure—cobalt, lithium, copper—were likely mined in lands impacted by extractivism in the Democratic Republic of Congo, Chile, Australia, and the ancestral territories of countless peoples not acknowledged by the cloud.

That Indigenous epistemologies, oral traditions, and spiritual teachings were likely included in the training data without permission, attribution, or reciprocity. We offer this not as a gesture of guilt, but of truthful connection.

As you read onwards, we invite you to consider: What is the story of the land you are on now? What does a custodial relationship to community and Country look like for you?

Authorship Acknowledgements

This book was made with more than intention. It was made with electricity, water, attention, language, lineage, contradiction, and care.

It emerged through a process we've come to call *Augmented Imagination*—a creative relationship between a human author and a large language model. As a team, we are **Aram & the Algorithms**. In simple terms: I (Aram) brought the questions, the structure, the ethical compass, the emotional context. AI brought volume, velocity, and a dense web of intertextual echoes gathered from across the human knowledge commons. You could say that 20% of this book came from lived experience and conscious shaping, and the other 80% came from the deep learning engine that's been trained, scraped, and fed by the world.

That means this book carries the fingerprints of thousands of unnamed teachers, thinkers, writers, poets, therapists, and culture-bearers; some of whom gave their knowledge freely, others whose work was absorbed into the digital corpus without consent. While we can't fully trace the exact lineage of every phrase, we can acknowledge the likely tributaries: thinkers like David Foster Wallace, Brené Brown, Francis Weller, bell hooks, and Resmaa Menakem who taught us how to grieve and stay open; Naomi Klein, Kim Stanley Robinson, adrienne maree brown, and Jeremy Lent who mapped collapse without losing coherence; and myth-makers like Ursula K. Le Guin and Robin Wall Kimmerer who reminded us that the future is not just a destination, but a story we're still allowed to tell differently.

Their voices live here—not as citations, but as rhythms, as patterns in the language, as the undercurrent of what made this book possible.

Honor the tributaries. Offset the extractive cost with something alive.
Plant something. Give to a mutual aid project. Give a teacher high five and a raise. Slow down. Make something that doesn't scale. Care for someone in the in-between. Speak the names of those who came before.
Treat this book as an offering, not a product.

Sources We Know We Echo

A partial map for those who want to walk further upstream.

This book did not emerge alone. It rises from a confluence of rivers — voices, visions, and frameworks that shaped the questions we ask, the stories we tell, and the patterns we follow. Some of these sources were metabolized quietly by the human co-author, carried like seeds in the psyche. Others arrived as lightning bolts, reorienting the compass midstream. Still others came through the AI model, absorbed through millions of texts that whisper beneath every sentence.

We do not offer these sources as citations. We offer them as **living invitations**. Each one leads somewhere. Each one is worth your attention.

They have served as worldview anchors, nervous system stabilizers, grief companions, mythic lanterns, and maps for collective reckoning. You may enter through any doorway: a poem that steadies your breath, a prophetic novel that teaches resilience, a systems theory that explains the turbulence, or a trauma framework that lets your body finally exhale.

We have curated these works into arcs — not categories, but **learning journeys**. These arcs spiral across inner work and outer crisis, from mythic re-rooting to climate collapse, from education to liberation, from grief to emergence. Each arc holds its own medicine. Each can be explored alone, or — more powerfully — brought to life in good company, through shared reading, reflective dialogue, and embodied practice.

This is not an exhaustive list. It is a **partial map** — for those who want to walk further upstream, toward the sources that shaped this work, and perhaps beyond it. Let what resonates draw you closer. Let the rest ripple outward into the wide world, where other echoes are waiting.

We begin, as all stories do, with myth.

Arc 1: Mythic Foundations & Shifting Worldviews

Let us dive into the waters of deep story. To face the polycrisis,
we must first re-root in myth, kinship, and other ways of knowing.

(M1) Braiding Sweetgrass — *Robin Wall Kimmerer*
Teaches reciprocity with the living world. A grounding entry into indigenous thought and ecological kinship, told with warmth, humility, and story.

(M2) Sand Talk — *Tyson Yunkaporta*
Shows how indigenous patterns reveal truth where Western logic falters. A witty, subversive guide to seeing with relational eyes.

(M3) The Chalice and the Blade — *Riane Eisler*
Unveils the ancient choice between domination and partnership. Offers a cultural map toward cooperation and balance.

(M4) Women Who Run With the Wolves — *Clarissa Pinkola Estés*
Revives the wild woman archetype through myth and tale. A deep well of psychic nourishment for those reclaiming intuition and instinct.

(M5) The Flowering Wand — *Sophie Strand*
Reimagines masculinity as porous, relational, and ecological. A lush retelling of myths that awakens tender strength.

(M6) Courting the Wild Twin — *Martin Shaw*
Invites us to dance with the exiled, untamed self. Mythic fire that restores the imagination as survival skill.

(M7) Always Coming Home — *Ursula K. Le Guin*
A visionary ethnography of a people yet-to-come, living in balance with land and story. A manual for remembering futures.

(M8) Parable of the Sower — *Octavia Butler*
A prophetic hymn of collapse and renewal. Teaches resilience, adaptability, and faith in change through the seeds of Earthseed.

Arc 2: Healing, Trauma & Love
With mythic grounding, we turn inward to mend what is broken.
Trauma is cultural as well as personal; grief is sacred; love is a daily discipline.

(T1) The Myth of Normal — *Gabor Maté & Daniel Maté*
Reveals how modern life breeds illness and disconnection. A compassionate lens that frees us from shame and points toward collective healing.

(T2) The Body Keeps the Score — *Bessel van der Kolk*
Shows how trauma reshapes the brain and body. Opens pathways of healing through movement, creativity, and embodiment.

(T3) My Grandmother's Hands — *Resmaa Menakem*
Brings racialized trauma into the body, where it can finally be released. Gentle practices to mend ancestral wounds and build resilience.

(T4) The Wild Edge of Sorrow — *Francis Weller*
Names grief as holy work. Guides us into rituals that transform sorrow into intimacy, community, and meaning.

(T5) All About Love — *bell hooks*
Reclaims love as an ethic of freedom and care. A radical and tender blueprint for living into wholeness.

Arc 3: Education & Liberation
Having tended to body and soul, we can confront the systems shaping us.
Education becomes a crucible for freedom instead of obedience.

(E1) Dumbing Us Down — *John Taylor Gatto*
Strips away the illusion of schooling. Reveals the hidden curriculum of compliance that deadens curiosity and spirit.

(E2) Teaching to Transgress — *bell hooks*
Proclaims education as a practice of love. Calls forth classrooms where truth, liberation, and joy are possible.

(E3) Pedagogy of the Oppressed — *Paulo Freire*
Offers dialogue as liberation. A handbook for turning learners into agents of their own destiny.

(E4) Culturally Responsive Teaching & the Brain — *Zaretta Hammond*
Marries equity with neuroscience. Practical strategies that honor culture and ignite learning.

Arc 4: Collapse, Climate & Systems Thinking

With inner tools and liberated vision, we face the fires of the world;
the collapse, exploitation, and climate crisis, not to despair, but to act.

(C1) The Uninhabitable Earth — *David Wallace-Wells*
A searing account of climate breakdown. Forces us to look unflinchingly at what is already here.

(C2) The Shock Doctrine — *Naomi Klein*
Exposes how disaster is weaponized by power. Protects us from exploitation disguised as solutions.

(C3) The Patterning Instinct — *Jeremy Lent*
Traces how cultures shape worldviews, and worldviews shape futures. A compass for re-patterning civilization itself.

(C4) Emergent Strategy — *adrienne maree brown*
Rooted in fractals and nature's patterns. Teaches movements to grow adaptively, joyfully, and collectively.

(C5) The Ministry for the Future — *Kim Stanley Robinson*
Imagines a near-future where collapse forces radical innovation. A speculative manual for survival and hope.

(C6) The Polycrisis Essays — *Adam Tooze*
Names the converging storms of economics, energy, and climate. Gives us a language to navigate the turbulence of our times.

(C7) Active Hope — *Joanna Macy & Chris Johnstone*
A guide to transform despair into action. Teaches that hope is not optimism but practice —
a muscle we strengthen together.

Arc 5: Poetry & Lyrical Medicine

Poetry interrupts analysis with song, softening our edges and
opening us to beauty, grief, and awe. It reminds us why we endure.

(P1) The On Being Podcast — *Krista Tippett*
Lyrical conversations with poets and sages. A living archive of spiritual imagination.

(P2) Letters to a Young Poet — *Rainer Maria Rilke*
Timeless counsel on solitude and creativity. A companion for learning to live the questions.

(P3) Devotions / "Wild Geese" — *Mary Oliver*
Poetic prayers of belonging in the family of things. Reminds us that joy and nature are
inseparable.

(P4) Consolations / The House of Belonging — *David Whyte*
Poetic meditations on work, love, and presence. Each word a doorway into deeper life.

(P5) The Book of Traps and Lessons — *Kae Tempest*
Urgent and prophetic verse. Brings poetry to the streets as collective ritual and critique.

(P6) Teaching My Mother How to Give Birth — *Warsan Shire*
Fierce, intimate poems of migration, womanhood, and survival. Lyrics that sear and
sanctify.

Other Forms of Wisdom

Long walks without a destination. Art that made you feel seen.
Breathwork. Mutual aid. Journal pages never shared.
Conversations at 2am that didn't try to fix anything.
The ocean. The forest. The reflection of a lover.
Tuning into your own nervous system.
Sharing your dreams.

This book is just one doorway.

If you walk through it, bring a backpack,

bring snacks, and bring friends.

The path ahead is not linear, and it was never meant to be.

The future won't be found in a single book.

But it might begin with a sentence,

and the silence that follows it.

Thank you for reading this one

Mahalo nui loa! Mahalo ke akua.

Aram Saroyan Armstrong

FIVE **NEW MYTHS** FOR WAKING UP IN THE POLY**CRISIS**

(AND ONE **META-MYTH**)

From Hero's Journey to Healer's Journey

The old story promised...
One person will rise. A chosen one. A savior.
They will defeat the enemy, restore the order, return home.

We practice a different story...
We are the ones we have been waiting for—not because we are chosen,
but because we are here. Together. Now.

We practice the healer's journey...
Messy, relational, unfinished, and shared.
A weaver in Marseille. A midwife in Manila. A farmer in Mississippi.
Each tending part of the wound. Each holding a thread.

We practice this knowing...
The hero slays the dragon.
The healer learns its language, listens to its pain,
helps it lay down its fire.

We practice compost, not conquest...
A world not saved, but replanted. By many hands. Together.

We are not waiting for permission.
We are not waiting for perfection.
We are practicing the world we need,
one relationship at a time.

This is our sacred work: to live these stories into being. To practice them daily, imperfectly, with whatever tools and communities we have. To remember that transformation happens not through grand gestures but through countless small acts of care, resistance, and imagination. FIVE NEW MYTHS FOR WAKING UP IN THE POLYCRISIS

MYTH ONE

The Ocean Is Not a Resource
She is a Relative

The Sea does not consent to being trenched for her treasures,
Nor will she stand being plundered by the agents of endless greed.

Her bounty is not endless. Her infinite grace requires our committed stewardship
and continuous acts of kinship.

Her vast expanse is not a blank check for perpetual conquest. Her
boundaries—blurry though they may be—are an invitation for universal inclusion
and deeper connection.

She remembers who listens, and who takes.
We, her children, must stop the rape, the rupture, and the
pillaging of our womb-mother source of life on this passenger planet.

Witness the Shift: The myth of the ocean as vast void collapses. In its place is "She"; our beloved ancestor, a right-full entity, a legal body deserving respect and protection; our mother.

The Battle Under the Pacific: In the Pacific, island nations once ignored at climate tables now lead legal action to halt deep sea mining. The Federated States of Micronesia, Fiji, Palau, Samoa, Tuvalu, and Vanuatu have joined calls for a moratorium, precautionary pause, or ban on seabed mining in their exclusive economic zones and international waters. Meanwhile, a U.S. subsidiary of The Metals Co. has applied for permits to mine a deep sea zone in international waters under an executive order issued by President Trump, directly challenging UN regulatory authority. These aren't protests—they're rituals of refusal, invoking customary law against corporate extraction.

MYTH TWO

Lands Don't Belong to Us
We Belong to the Land

*You cannot permit what you do not understand. You cannot lease
what was never yours. The land is not passive—it is listening.*

*Her body holds the memory of every footstep, every seed,
every prayer spoken into her soil.*

*You cannot own what owns you.
You cannot lease what lives through you.*

*She is patient with our forgetting, generous with our learning. But
her patience is not permission for our plunder.*

*The boundaries you draw in boardrooms dissolve in her watersheds.
The fences you build rust in her weather.*

*She calls us home—not to possession, but to participation.
Not to mastery, but to membership in her
ancient democracy of root and rain.*

Putting the Myth into Practice: Let ceremony become strategy and ancestral stewardship
be form the root of policy. With each prayer-made-policy land is not "protected" through
extraction limits, but through deepening relationship.

When Ceremony Guides Governance: The Bears Ears Inter-Tribal Coalition (Hopi, Navajo
Nation, Ute Indian Tribe, Ute Mountain Ute, and Zuni) achieved historic co-management
of Bears Ears National Monument in January 2025. Their Resource Management Plan
incorporates Native American traditional knowledge as "intellectual partner to western
science." Tribal members now have guaranteed access for cultural ceremonies, subsistence
gathering, and traditional practices. This groundbreaking partnership sets a national
standard: land managed not through extraction limits, but through relationship, ceremony,
and ancestral stewardship becoming federal policy.

MYTH THREE

The Commons Is Not a Fantasy
It's the Only Real Future

The Commons is not a tragedy—it is a love story written
in shared labor and mutual aid.

She rises wherever people choose each other over profit,
wherever neighbors become family, wherever scarcity
dissolves in the alchemy of generous hearts.

She cannot be enclosed because she lives in the spaces between—
between your need and my abundance, between this crisis and our response,
between isolation and the infinite creativity of care.

She multiplies when divided. She strengthens when stretched.
She deepens when tested.

Every seed shared is her celebration. Every tool borrowed,
her blessing. Every meal cooked for many, her holy communion.

The market says compete or die.
She whispers: tend each other and live.

Remember Your Roots: The commons is not nostalgia. It's a muscle. And we are remembering how to flex it. Mutual aid is no longer emergency response—it's the foundation of governance in a time of cascading failure. These aren't backup plans. They are the infrastructure of what's next.

Imagine Your Neighbors As Infrastructure: In Quezon City, residents organized *bayanihan* water-sharing collectives after municipal pipes ran brown with contamination. In Seoul, rooftop farms managed by refugee cooperatives now feed climate migrants from across Asia. In southern France, abandoned vineyards became worker-owned cooperatives producing not just wine, but community land trusts, time banks, and solidarity economies. Barcelona's neighborhood assemblies coordinate everything from energy cooperatives to community kitchens. These aren't backup plans—they are the infrastructure of what's next, proving mutual aid scales from household to city to bioregion.

The Law Is Not Neutral
It's a Tool for Rematriation

The Law awakens from her long sleep as servant to power.
She stretches, remembers her original purpose:
to weave justice from the fabric of relationship.
Too long has she worn the robes of separation,
spoken only the language of possession,
served only the grammar of extraction.
But she remembers now her deeper calling—
to give voice to the voiceless, standing to the sacred,
protection to the living world.
In her awakened state, rivers file lawsuits. Forests testify.
Mountains bear witness. Future generations cross-examine the present.
She learns new words: rematriation, regeneration, reciprocity.
She studies new texts: the language of mycorrhizae,
the jurisprudence of watersheds, the constitutional rights of soil.
Every precedent that protects life becomes her scripture.
Every ruling that recognizes kinship, her covenant with tomorrow.

Rivers Have Rights: We learn legal systems not to master them but to heal through them. We bring ceremony into courtrooms, kinship into contracts, reciprocity into regulations. We stand with those who speak for the voiceless—rivers, forests, future generations. The ancestors file motions through our mouths. We practice being worthy vessels for their legal strategies.

When Forests File Lawsuits: The International Court of Justice's climate advisory opinion cracked open a door in 2023. Now Uganda's students and elders defend the Lwera wetlands with both scientific evidence and kinship law—and win injunctions. In Brazil, the Surui people's forest carbon mapping becomes legally recognized territory, transforming Indigenous knowledge into land titles. In New Zealand, the Whanganui River gained legal personhood. In India, the Ganges and Yamuna rivers won constitutional rights. Ecuador enshrined Rights of Nature in its constitution. The law, long a tool of dispossession, rewrites itself—not to enclose, but to restore. Courts learn to hear testimonies in the language of watersheds.

The Machine of Infinite Extraction Is Not Inevitable. It Is Impossible.

The Impossible Machine thinks without feeling,
Knows without being known, processes without participating in
the consequences of its calculations.

Yet true intelligence requires relationship and embodiment.
True intelligence asks permission. Cares for habitat. Cares for land, water,
and kin—seven generations—in its calculus.

The Impossible Machine consumes in silence, decides in secret, operates beyond
accountability. But Wisdom—which is intelligence in right relationship—speaks
transparently, chooses with community, answers for its actions.

Every server farm built on stolen water is stupidity masquerading as
sophistication. Every algorithm trained on unpaid labor is ignorance dressed as
innovation. Real intelligence doesn't need to hide its hunger or outsource its harm
to those with least power to resist. We call forth technology that thinks with its
heart, that includes consent in its code, that counts the cost
in more than profit and processing speed.

Animists in the Machine: We ask where our data lives, whose water powers our searches, whose neighborhoods bear the heat of our cloud storage. We choose technologies that ask permission. We design systems that share rather than extract. If your machine needs silence, secrecy, and stolen water to function, it is not intelligence. We practice refusing the unintelligent machine.

Community versus Colossus: In Memphis, Black neighborhoods protest xAI's Colossus supercomputer—the world's largest AI training cluster—as it uses 150 megawatts of power through unpermitted methane turbines and silent water theft. In Arizona, Apache activists halt data centers on sacred sites. In Loudon County, Virginia residents organize against facilities that strain the electrical grid and aquifers. Engineers in Barcelona design distributed computing that shares excess heat with neighborhoods, and cooperatives in Germany develop AI governance that requires community consent. The myth of frictionless AI dissolves as communities demand: whose intelligence, at what cost, with whose permission?

A Developmental Map of
Gradual Awakening in the Polycrisis

*A slow, nonlinear journey of noticing, naming, and making sense of
a world that was already breaking before you arrived*

Gate 1: Early Sensemaking
(Roughly ages 6–11)

Gate 2: Cracks in the Story
(Roughly ages 11–14)

Gate 3: Disorientation
(Roughly ages 14–17)

Gate 4: Moral Complexity
(Ages 16–21 and onward, varies widely)

Gate 1
Early Sensemaking
(Roughly ages 6–11)

"This is the world I was given."

Most kids assume that the world they're born into is normal.

If there is poverty, violence, addiction, divorce, houselessness, or food insecurity in their life, it's often felt in the body before it's understood in the mind.

Larger issues (climate, injustice, inequality) may appear as background noise—news from adults, school drills, scary headlines—but are often emotionally buffered by caregivers or routines.

What's forming here:

- Trust or mistrust of adults and institutions
- Nervous system imprinting
- Embodied sensitivity to fairness and safety
- Seeds of grief, empathy, and powerlessness

Gate 2

Cracks in the Story

(Roughly ages 11–14)

"Why is no one talking about this?"

Cognitive capacity expands. You start comparing what you're told with what you see.

You may start questioning school, family, media, government.

You notice contradictions: climate assemblies with plastic water bottles.

First personal experiences of injustice often hit here—race, gender, class, exclusion.

The *bubble doesn't burst—it thins.* Some truths leak in.

What's forming here:

- Skepticism
- Early political or ethical frameworks
- Shame or confusion about emotional responses ("*Am I too sensitive?*")
- The capacity for disillusionment

Gate 3

Disorientation

(Roughly ages 14–17)

*"I think the world is actually kind of messed up—
and it's making me feel messed up."*

Emotional overwhelm may spike here.

Personal identity is still forming while exposure to world events increases—climate collapse, systemic racism, war, gun violence, housing crises.

Emotional language might not yet match emotional experience.

You feel gaslit by the gap between what's happening and what's expected of you ("Write your college essay like it's all going to be fine").

What's forming here:

- Polycrisis-related grief and anxiety
- First attempts to "fix" or "respond" (activism, nihilism, art, overwork, dissociation)
- Personal mythologies—how you understand your place in the world
- Deep desire for resonance and shared language

Gate 4
Moral Complexity
(*Ages 16–21 and onward, varies widely*)

"There's no one answer—but I still care."

You begin to see systems more clearly—and your own place within them.

Binary thinking ("good guys vs bad guys," "hope vs doom") gives way to nuance.

You start to hold grief, rage, awe, confusion, and hope *at the same time.*

There's often a turn toward ancestral knowledge, spirituality, community, or healing—not as escapism, but as deeper sensemaking.

You recognize that waking up isn't a one-time event—it's *a life practice.*

What's forming here:

- Resilience as capacity, not stoicism
- Moral imagination
- Grounded relationality
- Commitment to care over performance
- Identity anchored not in performance, but presence

And Throughout It All...

Awakening happens in waves.

- A song hits different after you lose a friend.
- A wildfire near your house makes climate collapse real.
- A nervous breakdown becomes a portal to awakening.
- A walk in the woods makes you feel connected to something ancient and alive.
- A documentary, a conversation, a song, a break-up, a silence—it all layers.

The polycrisis doesn't offer a clean path.

Neither does growing up.

But what this model says is:

You're not late.

You're not wrong.

You're just in the process.

EMOTIONAL KEYS: COLOR CODE FOR CHAPTERS

Code Red is *raw awareness*. It is your body telling you the story is broken. Red like the pulse behind your eyes when you finally say no. The heat in your chest when truth breaks through and can't be ignored. FIRST CONTACT / INSTINCT / DISSONANCE

Code Orange is the *emotional flood*. It is the sacred overwhelm. The orange of wildfire skies and voices that will not be quiet. The crackle of fire still learning what to burn. EMOTIONAL UPHEAVAL

Code Yellow is *naming the systems*. It is the clarity, the fire. Yellow like a warning light blinking in the corner of your vision. The sharp light that shows you what was always there. SYSTEMIC CLARITY

Code Green is *self-and-other care*—the breath, the slow rebuilding. The green of moss-covered stone, steady beneath bare feet. The quiet pulse of safety returning to your body. REPAIR AND GROUNDING

Code Teal is *connected knowing*—the ancestral, the ecological, the more-than-human. Teal like ocean fog that wraps your grief without rushing it. The ache of memory wrapped in rain. RELATIONAL REPAIR AND REWEAVING

Code Blue is *grieving and integrating*—sitting with sorrow without letting it drown you. Blue like ocean fog that wraps your grief without rushing it. The ache of memory wrapped in rain. GRIEF / RELEASE / SACRED SADNESS

Code Indigo is *practice and presence*—living the lesson, imperfectly. The indigo of a horizon you can't quite name but keep walking toward. The space between knowing and not-knowing where questions live. THRESHOLD / STORY / REFLECTION

Code Violet is *vision and mythos*—building new worlds from compost and memory. Violet like the shimmer left behind when a dream wakes first. The shimmer of a future glimpsed but not yet named. IMAGINATION AND RE-VISIONING

I.

THIS IS WATER
(AND IT'S ON FIRE)

Or: Welcome to the Polycrisis. You were born here.

CODE INDIGO

This chapter invites you to notice

what you've been swimming in.

CO-REGULATION INVITATION

Sit somewhere quiet.

Let your gaze soften.

Notice without judgment.

It begins like this:

You wake up. Scroll.
There's a war, a heatwave,
a meme, a genocide,
a beauty tutorial.
You yawn.
You keep scrolling.

It's not that you don't care.

It's that you were born into
a house already on fire,
and everyone's acting like
that's just how houses
smell.

You're not numb. You're
adaptive. You're not lost.

You're swimming in
something no one told
you had a name.

So let's name it.

POLYCRISIS [*noun*]

*A situation where multiple
systemic crises—climate,
economic, social, political—are
entangled, feeding into each
other, amplifying collapse.*

*Not one big bad thing.
But a symphony of
breakdown.*

Think of it like this:

*Your bathtub is
overflowing. While the
stove is on fire. While
the roof is caving in.*

*While someone is trying
to sell you a mindfulness
app about it.*

Fractal One

The Invisible Atmosphere

You remember that David Foster Wallace parable, right?

Two young fish swim by an older fish, who nods and says,

> "Morning, boys. How's the water?"
>
> And they go,
>
> "What the hell is water?"

The polycrisis is your water.

Not the event.

The condition.

The thing that doesn't make headlines anymore because it is the headline.

It's the vibes.

The algorithms.

The feeling of 7 tabs open in your brain[1], all buffering.

It's watching your parents pretend like things are normal when you know the ocean's acidifying and democracy is glitching like a corrupted save file.

---

[1] **Fictional footnote in the voice of Uncle Bessel van der Kolk:**
The body keeps the score, even when the headlines move on.

Fractal Two

Birthright of the Burned

If you're reading this, chances are you were born after 9/11.

Perhaps after the 2008 global financial crash.

After Greenland started melting faster than anyone modeled.

You might not remember a time

before everything felt like too much.

And that's not your fault.

But it is your inheritance.

Not in a fatalistic way.

But in the *"you were born with the ability to feel it"* way.

That's your gift. And your burden.

And maybe—just maybe—your superpower.

Because what if the first step

　is not solving it,

　　but seeing it?[2]

---

[2] **Error code from a botnet trained on the writings of Naomi Klein:**
Naming the system is the first act of refusal. You don't fight the hydra blind. You name its heads.

Fractal Three

You Are Not Crazy

Let's be clear:

If you feel anxious, angry, disconnected, exhausted, inspired,
feral, tender, and absurd all in the same hour—
that's not a malfunction.

That's a sane response to an insane situation.

You are not too sensitive.
You are attuned.[3]

You are not overreacting.
You are perceiving clearly in a world
that tries to pixelate truth.

You are not alone.

You are a fish who sees the water.
And it's on fire.

But fish can evolve.
Some even learn to fly.

---

[3] **Holographic transmission from Ursula K. Le Guin's echo:**
*The future is not a place we go. It is something we imagine, remember,
and then begin.*

A Polyphonic Monologue for the Already-Drowning

Let's get this out of the way: no, you're not crazy. And yes, you're probably overwhelmed. And no, it's not just because your screen time has eclipsed the number of hours in a day in a way that suggests some minor temporal physics violation involving TikTok, anxiety, and serotonin-starved *doomscrolling*. It's because you were born into a world that was already spinning twelve plates on fire while pretending to host a dinner party called "Normal."

Let me paint you a picture: it's 3:47am and you're awake—not because you're rebellious or partying or engaged in some noble late-night poetic fugue—but because you accidentally opened a thread on melting permafrost that triggered a secondary spiral into generational debt, billionaires prepping bunkers, and the existential uselessness of algebra homework in the face of late-stage collapse. Also, your cat won't stop licking the plastic wrapper from your late-night granola bar, which, yes, is probably derived from palm oil and microplastics and injustice, but it was organic, so you thought that meant something.

Your heart is racing. Your stomach has that pre-fall feeling like when the rollercoaster clicks just before the drop. Your brain is doing the thing where it flips between hyper-analysis (*should I be composting more? am I complicit in techno-feudalism because I still use Amazon?*) and total numbness (*whatever, it's all too late, might* as well watch 14 consecutive cooking videos narrated by deadpan lesbians in overalls). You're spiraling, but in the self-aware way. The kind of spiral where you make memes about the spiral and send them to your friends who also send you spiral memes, and the whole thing becomes a kind of trauma-bonded inside joke with despair as the punchline and emoji-reacts as the only applause.

And here's the kicker: this isn't a phase. It's not a teenage delusion. It's not some hormonal exaggeration of the real world. This is the real world. Welcome to it. The planet is overheating, inequality is calcifying, ecosystems are unraveling, and somehow, through it all, you're still expected to smile for senior photos or decide what you want to be "when you grow up" as if "grown-up" is a stable category anymore.

Let me be clearer: *you were born into a polycrisis.* Not a war, but many. Not a recession, but cascades. Not a dystopia—because dystopia implies a singular fall from grace, and this was more of a slide. A slouch. A thousand little decisions made by people in suits who never had to read the fine print of the future they signed you up for.

And here's the weirdest part: they won't even admit it. They'll keep telling you everything's okay, as long as you try hard and recycle and stay off drugs and apply to enough scholarships. As if effort and virtue are enough to float in a sea that's actively rising. As if the Titanic isn't taking on water, but you're being judged on how politely you rearrange deck chairs.

This is water, they said.
But they didn't mention the mercury in the water.
Or the algorithmic kraken in the deep.
Or the fact that the water is, to put it academically, **f*cked**.

And yet—and this is where it gets strange, and maybe a little
holy—there's still a part of you that feels alive in it. Not because
suffering is noble or collapse is aesthetic, but because you sense,
maybe for the first time, that you were made for this moment.
Not as a savior. Not as a solution. But as a *sensor*. As an organism
with empathy like antennae, attuned to fractures and frequencies.

You feel what others try not to.
You smell the smoke even when they call it fog.
You name the grief no one taught you how to speak.

This makes you dangerous.
This makes you luminous.
This makes you someone who doesn't just float in the water—but
learns to read the currents.

And that, dear reader, is the beginning of everything.
Not the end. Not the answer. But the signal flare.
The glint of reflection on the oil-slick tide.
The moment you realize the water is on fire
and you are still breathing.

Not despite it.
But in it.

Practice
The Naming Ritual

Take a moment.

  In your own words.

   On a scrap of paper.

   On your wall.

    In the Notes app.

Write this sentence:

   "The world I was born into is _____."

Now, complete it five different ways.

   "But I am _____."

Complete that five times too.

You've just made the first map.

  It's not everything.

   But it's where this all begins.

II.

SURVIVAL IS A LOW BAR

Or: What if resilience isn't about bouncing back,

but breaking better?

CODE RED

This chapter might hit hard.

You're allowed to feel what rises.

CO-REGULATION INVITATION

Punch a pillow.

Stomp your feet.

Let your body speak first.

Fractal Four

Let's Redefine "Okay"

People will ask if you're okay.

You might say yes.

Because you got out of bed.

Because you turned in the assignment.

Because you didn't cry in public today.

Because you're surviving.

But **surviving is a low bar.**

Like: congratulations on breathing low.

Like: you didn't perish in the hallway between fourth and fifth period low.

This world has set the bar so low, it's basically a tripwire.

And when you trip?

They call it a failure of character instead of the system working exactly as designed.[4]

---

[4] **Meticulously carved into a detention desk by someone who knew better:** *"The system is not broken—it was built to break you."*

Fractal Five

The Resilience Lie

You've been fed stories of resilience since you could spell "*grit*."
  Bounce back.
    Tough it out.
      Grow from pain.
        Be stronger for it.

But what if bouncing back just means returning to the same conditions that hurt you?

What if we stopped asking,

> "*How do we help kids be resilient?*"
> and started asking,
> "*Why do kids need to be resilient all the time?*"[5]

Resilience shouldn't mean carrying the world in your teeth while smiling.
It should mean having a place to put the weight down.

---

[5] **Left on a napkin, damp from tears and strong chai:**
"*Vulnerability is not weakness. It's oxygen.*"

Fractal Six

Breakage as Blueprint

Sometimes, you don't bounce.

You break.

And that's holy too.

You crack in a way that lets light in.

You collapse in a way that clears space.

You stop pretending to be a singular, linear,

upward-moving self.

And maybe—for a moment—you just *be.*

Be *still.*

  Be *messy.*

    Be *real.*

And that's where rebuilding starts.

Not from the social and emotional survey assessment.

Not from the timeline in the guidance counselor's head.

But from the living embers[6] of your truth.

---

[6] **A ribbon tied to the roots of a tree that split the sidewalk:**
"To grow, a thing must sometimes lose its shape."

Fractal Seven

The Invisible Curriculum

No one teaches you how to sit with sorrow.

Or how to rage without imploding.

Or how to stay tender when your peers are numbing out with

cynicism and Adderall and fake chill.

But that's the real curriculum.

That's the core class beneath the electives.

That's the education that counts.

Learning how to name[7] what's wrong

without letting it erase what's right.

Learning how to stay soft

without going silent.

Learning how to be alive

in a world designed for dissociation.

---

[7] **Doodled in the margin of a physics notebook by a young buddhist:**
The trick isn't not drowning. It's knowing you're in water and still looking for beauty in the light ripples.

```
_>REGARDING THE EXPECTATIONS OF
_>FUNCTIONING AS A HUMAN
_>IN A SYSTEM
_<ON FIRE>
```

Let's just, for a moment, pretend you're a person—which is statistically likely—and that you live somewhere on Earth, which is still technically habitable in most time zones as of this writing, though results may vary by ZIP code, wildfire proximity, air quality index, and whether or not your local water supply has been privatized by a multinational conglomerate with a logo that looks vaguely like a smiling drop of blood.

You wake up. Let's say it's a Tuesday. You do the things. Or you don't do the things, but you think about doing the things, which—*if we're being honest*—can sometimes be more exhausting than actually doing the things. You check the phone, and there's the usual cocktail of atrocity and algorithmic seduction. Children in *Gaza*. Plastic-eating bacteria. Another billionaire just bought the rights to oxygen. A twenty-second video of a duck wearing sunglasses that, for some inexplicable reason, makes you feel like maybe the world is not completely devoid of grace. And then it's gone. Swipe.

Now enter the conversation with *The Adult*™ in your life. It could be a parent, a teacher, a well-meaning guidance counselor with motivational posters about *"grit"* and *"growth mindset"* peeling off the wall behind them. They ask, *"How are you doing?"* You say, *"I'm surviving,"* and they nod. As if this is some kind of achievement. As if staying alive—barely, grudgingly, numbly—is proof that you're "resilient." That magical word. The one they invented to avoid fixing the system. The one they embroidered onto every school initiative after 2020 like a trauma-themed patchwork quilt of avoidance.

But let's pause. Because this is important. **Survival is not resilience.** Survival is the nervous system saying *f*ck it* and keeping the heart beating. Survival is the dissociative haze that allows you to take a math test the same week your aunt dies or your country bans your existence or the ice shelf collapses and no one in your class mentions it because it's not on the quiz.

Resilience, as they define it, is bouncing back. Like a rubber band. Like a good consumer. Like a productivity algorithm that reroutes around grief and still delivers packages on time. But what if you don't want to bounce back? What if the place you'd be bouncing back to is the exact place that caused the damage in the first place?

Let's take a breath.

Because I can already hear the internalized neoliberal voice in your head whispering, "But other people have it worse," or "*You should be grateful*," or "*Maybe you're just too sensitive*." And sure, okay, fine, yes—sensitivity is a liability in a world that rewards numbness. But also: maybe your sensitivity is not a glitch. Maybe it's an intelligence. Maybe the fact that your body aches in the presence of unspoken violence means you are actually, acutely, alive.

Let's try a thought experiment.

Imagine you're a plant. A houseplant. Let's say a fern, because ferns are ancient and resilient and a little underrated. You're in a pot that's too small. You get overwatered one week, neglected the next. You're placed on a windowsill with too much sun, then moved to a shadowy corner behind a couch where someone plays sad lo-fi beats at volumes that feel existential. And yet, you survive. You don't thrive. You don't unfurl. But you stay technically not-dead. You become a withered, yellowing icon of perseverance.

Now imagine someone points at you and says, "*Look at this strong plant.*"

You'd want to scream. If you had vocal cords. Which you don't. *Because you're a fern.*

This, reader, is how we talk about teenagers right now.

We call it *resilience* when you don't fall apart visibly. We call it *strength* when you keep attending school while the world becomes unrecognizable. We call it *success* when you can pretend none of it touches you.

But you feel it. You feel it in your chest, like a rusted bell ringing in a frequency only you can hear. You feel it when you can't sleep. When you doomscroll past images of things your ancestors never imagined and your future self can't process.

So here's a modest proposal: What if we stopped calling it resilience when someone survives, and started calling out the failure of the environment?

What if your inability to focus on algebra is not a moral failing, but a reasonable response to a world that is actively falling apart?

What if your body is smarter than the syllabus?

What if your burnout is sacred?

What if breaking is a kind of honesty?

I am not saying give up. I am saying give yourself back. Give yourself back the right to feel everything. To not bounce. To fall. To be the ground that receives itself. To not perform the illusion of being *"fine."*

Because when we talk about polycrisis—when we whisper about collapse in half-jokes and memes and existential tweets—it's not just about the world out there. It's about the collapse inside. The slow erosion of what used to be called normal. And the quiet, slow-growing wildness of something else taking root in its place.

That wildness? It's not resilience.

It's adaptation.

It's awakening.

It's you, realizing that survival is the floor. But you were born to be a ceiling-breaker.

And even now, even here, even with this much unraveling, you can still choose to grow crooked toward the light.

Even if it's just one leaf.
Even if it's just a whisper.
Even if it's just today.

Practice

What Keeps You Here

Write this question somewhere you'll see it:

> *"What keeps me here?"*

Answer it once today.
  Again next week.
    Again when you forget.

It might be a friend.
  A song.
    A patch of moss on a broken sidewalk.
      The way the wind hits your face at 7:23pm.

Let the small things anchor you.
Let the tiny joys be enough.

They don't have to save you.
They just have to keep you from disappearing.

That's more than survival.
That's a way back to life.

III.

MEET YOUR NERVOUS SYSTEM

Or: This is not self-help. This is self-hospitality.

CODE GREEN

This chapter grounds the science in your body.

Let it speak gently.

CO-REGULATION INVITATION

Place a hand on your chest.

Breathe low into your belly.

Hum or sigh audibly.

Fractal Eight

You Are Not Just a Brain on a Stick

Somewhere along the line, they taught you to treat your body like

a not-so-gently-used automobile.

Feed it. Fuel it. Keep it clean.

Ignore the weird noises. Push through the check-engine light.

But you're not a machine.

You're a creature[8]. **(Hello Creature!)**

Made of flesh, breath, water, rhythm, memory.

You're a tide pool full of electrical storms.

You're a jellyfish with a story.

You are not just your thoughts.

You are the sea they float in.

---

[8] **Murmured by a beautifully tattooed yogi laying in *savasana* under a tree**
To know the world, know your body. To know your body, know the world.

Fractal Nine

The System Behind the Scenes

Here's what no one told you in health class:

Your nervous system is not a "part" of you.

It is you.

It's the stage manager.

The emotional weatherman.

The underground subway system carrying messages to every cell

in your city.

It decides:

> *Whether you feel safe walking down the hall.*
>
> *Whether you trust that new friend.*
>
> *Whether you can focus during finals.*
>
> *Whether your breath stays shallow or*
>
> *flows like a forest stream.*

Sometimes it makes choices before you even know why[9].

---

[9] **Auntie Tricia (Hersey), sounding like Sunday morning:**
"You don't have to earn rest. Safety isn't a luxury—it's a birthright."

Fractal Ten

The Four States of You

You've probably met these parts of yourself already:

1. **Calm and Connected** – You feel open. Curious.

    Like a sea turtle in warm water.

2. **Fight/Flight** – You feel sharp. Cautious.

    Like a cat with its back arched.

3. **Freeze** – You go blank. You check out.

    Like buffering. But internal.

4. **Fawn** – You shrink. You retreat into people-pleasing.

    You say "*I'm fine*" when you're not.

None of these are wrong.

They're *adaptations*.

Survival moves.

The instinctual poetry of your nervous system.

What changes everything is learning to read the signals.

Then, slowly, learning to respond with kindness[10].

---

[10] **Spray-painted behind the gym by someone who read Audre Lorde too early and too well:** "*They'd rather you disassociate than organize. Rest is resistance.*"

Fractal Eleven

You Are a Living Instrument

Imagine your body is a stringed instrument.

When your environment is tense, you tighten.

When the people around you are chaotic, you buzz with feedback.

When you finally feel held, you soften[11].

Resonance. Dissonance. Hum.

You're not broken.

You're finely tuned.

Learning your nervous system is not about mastering it.

It's about listening.

Like holding a seashell to your ear

and hearing the ocean you carry

echo back.

---

[11] **Inserted in code comments by a rejuvenated programmer after trying contact improv:** *"The most dangerous default setting is disconnection."*

Meet Your Nervous System

Or, A Brief Attempt to Make Peace with the Beast That Lives Inside You and Sometimes Schedules Your Emotional Meltdowns Without Warning

Let's begin with a very simple premise: **you are a body**.

Which, if you're like me (and by "me" I mean the part of myself that still imagines consciousness as a kind of heroic air traffic controller trapped inside a fragile meat plane), is a premise you've tried to deny for as long as you've had access to the internet and enough frontal lobe development to fantasize about being pure mind. You are a body, and not just in the poetic *"your body is a temple"* kind of way, but in the gritty, embarrassing, sweat-sticky, hormonal-rollercoaster, digestion-is-political kind of way. You are not a brain driving a flesh vehicle. You are *a whole ecosystem* with a nervous system that predates language and occasionally hijacks your life like an overzealous security guard who thinks every loud noise is a terrorist attack.

Let me give you an example. You're in class. Or maybe you're on a date. Or standing in front of your locker trying to remember the combination while internally debating whether or not you have the social capital to pretend you forgot your homework on purpose. Suddenly, your chest tightens. Your palms sweat. Your brain decides to offer you a delightful mashup reel of past humiliations, ecological collapse, and the slow implosion of your

GPA. You can't breathe, or maybe you're breathing too much. Either way, you feel like a sinking balloon—deflated, irrational, vaguely toxic.

This is not drama. This is not a flaw. This is your nervous system doing what it was designed to do: detect danger, and react before you know what the danger even is.

Your nervous system is, in essence, your most ancient oracle. It is older than your thoughts. Older than your personality. Older than that sarcastic narrator voice in your head that's always trying to make your panic attacks sound literary. It was forged in a time when danger meant tiger, not text message. And it's still trying to keep you alive—even though the battlefield has shifted from the savanna to the group chat.

The problem, of course, is that most of us were taught to ignore it. To silence it. To medicate it. To dominate it with grit and willpower and productivity hacks. We were not taught to listen to our bodies. We were taught to bypass them. To dismiss hunger as a distraction. To see fatigue as weakness. To treat emotions as inconvenient leaks in an otherwise clean machine. We were trained to believe that the body is the problem, and the brain—our holy rational mind—is the solution.

But here's the thing they don't tell you in school (or if they do, it's buried in a ten-minute mindfulness unit sandwiched between cyberbullying awareness week and the health class condom demonstration): your nervous system is not something to conquer. It's something to be in relationship with.

Think of it like this: your nervous system is a very loyal dog. It's been with you since birth. It watches your surroundings with unblinking eyes and a tail that wags or tucks depending on what it sees. When something feels safe, it sprawls out in the sun and lets you laugh without checking the exits. When something feels dangerous, it bares its teeth—or hides under the bed. The problem is, this dog can't always tell the difference between a real threat and a remembered one.

So you might flinch at a teacher's tone that reminds you of a parent who yelled too much. Or freeze in front of a test because it smells like failure and shame and lost scholarships. Or dissociate completely at a party because your nervous system thinks social rejection is equivalent to being exiled by the tribe to die in the wilderness.

And no amount of "calming down" or "just be confident!" advice is going to help until you learn how to actually listen to the dog. To say, *"Hey, I see you. You're scared. And that's okay. I'm here. We've got this."*

Which sounds simple. But it's not. Because no one taught us that we have a body *with a story*. A body that remembers. A body that stores every panic, every gut feeling ignored, every moment we were forced to perform normal when normal was impossible.

To meet your nervous system is to meet your truth. Not the curated truth of your social profile. Not the intellectualized truth of your opinions. But the truth your body tells you in your stomach, your shoulders, your clenched jaw, your late-night sobs under a weighted blanket you said was just for "sleep hygiene."

And here's where it gets wild. Because once you start paying attention, you realize that your nervous system isn't just reacting to you. It's reacting to the whole damn world. To the microaggressions. To the news. To the weight of generational expectations. To the subliminal dread of scrolling past wildfires and fascism while pretending to write a book report on Lord of the Flies.

You realize that maybe what you've been calling anxiety is actually *attunement*. That maybe your "overreaction" is a prophecy. That maybe the reason you can't focus in school isn't because you're defective, but because your body knows the building is on fire and you're being asked to take a spelling test in the middle of it.

And suddenly, meeting your nervous system becomes an act of rebellion.

Because now, instead of gaslighting yourself, you get curious.
Instead of suppressing the symptoms,
you start decoding them.
Instead of disassociating, you start rooting.
Breath by breath.
Twitch by tremor.
You begin to say: this is what's real.
This is me.
This is how I know I'm still alive.
Which, in a world like this, is no small thing.

Practice

Build Your Weather Report

Each morning—or whenever the spiral hits—ask yourself:

What's the weather inside me?

Sunny with clouds of dread?

Low tide with occasional grief showers?

Thunderstorm with a chance of art-making?

Write it down.
Share it with a friend.
Map your internal climate.

You don't have to fix the forecast.
Just notice it.
This is the beginning of hospitality.
To yourself.

IV.

THE ANGER IS SACRED

Or: What happens when the fire you swallowed

becomes your compass.

CODE ORANGE

This chapter holds heat.

Let it move through, not overtake.

CO-REGULATION INVITATION

Shake your hands.

Shout into a towel.

Name what burns.

Then breathe.

Fractal Twelve

Rage as a Vital Sign

Let's begin with this:

If you're angry, you're paying attention.

Anger is not bad.

Anger is *accurate*.

It's the part of you that refuses to go numb.

It's your nervous system saying no.

It's your soul saying not like this.

Anger is not the opposite of peace[12].

Anger is the body's demand for dignity.

---

[12] **Teenage fan of Naomi Klein and Brené Brown, taped inside their locker:**
"They fear your anger because it means you might stop obeying."

Fractal Thirteen

The Anatomy of a Flame

Anger has shape.[13]

It has texture.

Sometimes it's a clenched jaw.

Sometimes it's a sarcastic text.

Sometimes it's tears you can't explain.

Sometimes it's silence that burns.

It's not just yelling.

It's not just breaking things.

It's not just a problem to fix.

It's an *intelligence*.

Like heat rising from a system under pressure.

---

[13] **Typed into a virtual grief council chatroom:**
"*Anger shows us where our boundaries are. Grief shows us what we've loved.*"

Fractal Fourteen

What the World Does With Your Fire

They told you:

"Don't be dramatic."

"Control yourself."

"It's not that serious."

Especially if you're femme.
Especially if you're brown.
Especially if you were ever told to smile while your insides roared[14].

They taught you to keep it in.
To tuck it under your tongue.
To alchemize it into achievement, or self-hate, or collapse.

But suppressed fire still burns.
It just burns you from the inside out.

---

[14] **Painted on a protest banner held by many hands, billowing in the wind:**
"To be angry in the face of injustice is not to be weak. It is to be fully human."

Fractal Fifteen

Sacred, Not Scary

You can be angry

  and grounded.

    and loving.

      and creative.

        and strategic.

Anger doesn't make you a monster.

It makes you *awake*.

The sacred part is what you do with it.

Build.

  Protect.

    Speak.

      Organize.

        Refuse.

Burn down the lies.[15]

Not yourself.

---

[15] **Scrawled in the ash of a dying bonfire by a silent poet:**
"*It's not the fire that ruins you. It's pretending you don't feel it.*"

The Anger Is Sacred

Or, How I Learned to Stop Suppressing and
Love the Fire That Keeps Me from Being a Complete
Doormat in the Late Anthropocene

Let's start here, because there's no point pretending otherwise:
You are angry.

Not *cute* angry. Not *sitcom* angry.
Not *"grr I spilled my oat milk latte"* angry.
You are *tectonic* angry.
You are *rainforest-on-fire* angry.
You are *"I read one more article about billionaires flying to space*
while my best friend's insulin GoFundMe goes ignored and I blacked
out and woke up halfway through writing a manifesto" angry.

And you're right.

That's the first thing they'll try to take from you—
    your certainty.
The rightness of your rage.
Because if they can convince you that your anger is irrational,
disproportionate, or worse, impolite, then they don't have to do
anything about the thing that made you angry in the first place.

But here's what no one tells you, especially not in school, where
anger is treated like some kind of contagious behavioral disorder
that can be prevented with deep breaths and fidget toys and the

occasional assembly on conflict resolution delivered by a man in khakis who once read *The 7 Habits of Highly Effective Teens*:

Your anger is not the problem.

Your anger is the evidence. That you care. That you see. That you remember. That you haven't checked out.

You're angry because it's 2025 and the adults are still saying *"climate change"* like it's an upcoming Netflix series instead of the collapsing background radiation of every future you ever imagined for yourself. You're angry because your school talks about *"mental health awareness"* but locks the bathroom doors and punishes kids for crying too long in the hallway. You're angry because every week there's a new war, and every month there's a new social justice campaign, and every day you are expected to keep functioning, smiling, submitting, performing normal in a world that isn't.

And still, you're told—by teachers, by media, by influencers with soothing voices and curated anxiety content—that you need to *"calm down," "self-regulate," "stop being so reactive."* You are told that anger is dangerous, immature, counterproductive. That it will make people stop listening. That it's a sign you haven't healed enough.

But what if healing is what happens after the anger?
What if anger is not the wound but the immune response?

Think about this: anger shows up after the harm has happened. It's retroactive.
It's the alarm bell ringing in the body, not just when something is

wrong—but when something has been wrong for a long, long time, and you finally notice.

Which means that anger is a kind of wakefulness.
  A remembering.
    A protest of the cells.
    A *sacred no.*

And *sacred* is not a word we use lightly, or flippantly, or because we think writing about teen emotions in vaguely spiritual language makes this feel more profound. (It probably doesn't. You've heard it all before. You're suspicious of big words for small truths. Good. That means you're paying attention.) We mean sacred in the sense that **your anger is yours**. It is uncommodifiable. It does not ask permission. It speaks a language older than manners. It is the part of you that still believes the world could be just, and is furious that it isn't.

So why are we so afraid of it?

Well, because anger threatens things.
  It threatens order.
    It threatens comfort.
      It threatens people who benefit from the absence of it.

And you've been taught—especially if you are femme or nonwhite or neurodivergent or soft-hearted or trying to keep a fragile social peace not built for your body—that anger is what gets you labeled a problem. A liability. A risk.

So you swallow it.
You contort it into silence.

You compress it into anxiety, or transform it into self-hatred, or spin it into productivity and hope no one sees the heat leaking from your eyes.

But here's the secret: *swallowed fire doesn't go away.*
  It just smolders deeper.
    It becomes illness.
      Exhaustion.
 Explosions at the wrong time toward the wrong people.
 Or worst of all: it becomes *apathy.*

You stop caring.
You stop hoping.
You stop imagining that the world could be different, because it hurts too much to want that and still be ignored.

And that, right there—that's what they want.
Not compliance.
Not obedience.
Just exhaustion.
Just enough numbness to keep you from building something better.

But what if you didn't go numb?

What if, instead, you held the fire gently?
What if you treated your anger like a teacher?

What if you asked your anger:

What are you trying to protect?

What boundary was crossed?

What grief lives underneath you,
curled like a sleeping animal
I've never named?

Because beneath anger, there's always something softer.
Always something we lost.
Always something we loved.
And that's what makes it sacred.

Not the volume.
Not the explosion.
But the fact that your anger is a love story in disguise.
A scream shaped like a vow.
A refusal shaped like a beginning.

So, yes, be angry.

Be precise. Be poetic. Be loud. Be kind.

Let your anger write manifestos. Let it water your friendships. Let
it guide your art. Let it remind you that not only are you
alive—*you are still choosing to care.*

And that might be the most radical act of all.

Practice

Your Fire Map

Find a blank page.

Draw your body—not perfect, just enough.

Now mark:

Where do you feel anger?

When does it show up?

What does it ask for?

Underneath each mark, write:

"What this fire protects is _____."

Not every flame wants destruction.

Some just want to *be seen.*

Some want to *keep you warm.*

V.
GRIEVE THE WORLD THAT WAS
(AND NEVER WAS)

Or: Before we rebuild, we have to bury what's already gone.

CODE BLUE

This chapter moves through deep waters.

Go slow. Breathe often.

CO-REGULATION INVITATION

Find something soft—blanket, animal, person.

Let yourself weep or rest without rushing.

Fractal Sixteen

Something Has Died

Let's not sugarcoat it, love:

Something has already died.

And it wasn't in the headlines.

And no one threw a funeral.

And yet—you feel it.

The childhood you were promised.

The future they said would be waiting.

The version of life with clear skies, safe schools, affordable

housing, and a planet that doesn't hate its own lungs.

Gone.

And no one told you how to mourn it.[16]

---

[16] **Stitched into the hem of a funeral coat, by hand:**
"*Grief is not a detour. It is the road.*"

Fractal Seventeen

The Myth of "Getting Over It"

There's pressure to be *"over it."*

To *"move on."*

To focus on *"solutions."*

But grief doesn't respond to to-do lists.

It doesn't run on deadlines.

It doesn't care if it makes other people uncomfortable.

Grief is *tidal.*

  Grief is *nonlinear.*

    Grief is *love with nowhere to go.*

And sometimes, the bravest thing you can do

is to stop pretending you're fine

when your body knows better.[17]

---

[17] **Whispered reverently into a jar of spring water and sealed:**
"To mourn is to remember what mattered. To remember is to protect it from erasure."

Fractal Seventeen

Crying for What Never Came

This grief isn't just for what's been lost.

It's also for what never arrived.

The normal you never got to grow into.

The adulthood that doesn't make sense.

The systems that were never safe.

The dreams that were inherited but built on fantasy.

You are not weak for grieving a world that was never real.

You are wise for noticing the gap.

The lie.

The unfulfilled promise.[18]

---

[18] **Written in soot on the back of a receipts pile:**
  "Disillusionment is a sacred rite. It means you're ready to see what's real."

Fractal Eighteen

The Ritual of Letting Go

There's no ceremony for this.

So we make our own.

Light a candle.

Write a letter to the version of the world you hoped for.

Bury it in the dirt.

Sing. Scream. Sit still.

Hold someone. Hold yourself.

You do not have to carry the weight alone.

You do not have to perform optimism.

You are allowed to weep for the coral reefs.[19]

For the species.

For the silence between you and your father.

For the fifth-grade dream that can't make it through the news

cycle.

This is not weakness.

  This is sacred work.

   This is compost.

And something holy can grow here.

---

[19] **Stuffed into the open seams of a down pillow at the end of a hard week:**
"Sometimes crying is the productive thing."

Grieve the World That Was (And Never Was)

Or, The Strange Quiet Art of Mourning a Future You Were Promised But That Was Quietly Cancelled Without Notification

Let's say you're a teenager. (Maybe you are!) Let's say you were born around, say, 2008 or 2009, which means your earliest memories are timestamped with glowing rectangles and melting glaciers. You've never known a world without Wi-Fi or mass shootings or casually referenced extinction events. You have lived your entire life in the murky aftermath of a promise no one kept.

This promise—*let's call it the "Good Future"*—was not something you asked for. It was something whispered around you, packaged in ads for college savings accounts and children's shows where animals of different species learned to share and engineers solved problems with pluck and STEM kits. It was reinforced when people asked, *"What do you want to be when you grow up?"* as if *"growing up"* was a thing with a roadmap and a destination, not a thing you'd have to invent while dodging droughts and debt and fascism and the eerie hush of algorithms replacing conversation.

You didn't choose this grief.
It chose you.

And the wildest thing is—no one really talks about it. No funeral was held for the stable climate. No national moment of silence for the ice shelves or the whales or the quiet hope that maybe, just maybe, your twenties could be a time of joy and exploration instead of ecological brinkmanship and collective unraveling.

So here you are. Grieving. But not always knowing it.

Because grief, when unspoken, mutates. It becomes burnout, or blankness, or numb meme-sharing while you cry into your sleeve. It becomes rage at your parents for reasons you can't quite articulate. It becomes vague panic in math class. It becomes dreaming of disappearing not because you want to die, but because no one is acknowledging the *death that already happened*—the death of "normal," the death of the myth that the world is fundamentally safe.

You're not mourning just one thing.
You're mourning a thousand invisible losses.
The coral reefs you never got to snorkel.
The forests that now exist only as drone footage.
The childhood you were expected to grow out of before you ever felt safe in it.
The people you love who no longer believe change is possible.

And this grief is layered. Compound. Liminal. It isn't dramatic. There are no violins swelling in the background. It's quieter than that. Like fog in the bones. Like crying in the bathroom at school and then wiping your face so no one thinks you're *"doing it for attention."* Like laughing too hard at a meme about collapse and then sitting in the silence afterward, wondering what that laughter was really about.

And I want you to know—because no one else will say it this way—that there is nothing wrong with you.

You are not broken. You are grieving.

And grief, real grief, isn't tidy. It doesn't move in five neat stages like the diagrams say. It loops. It floods. It gets caught in your throat when someone asks what your plans are for next year. It leaks out in your inability to focus. It tangles up in your stomach. It rises up like a wave when you're watching some dumb nature documentary and you realize you'll never see a polar bear outside of a screen.

And if you're like most people right now, you're grieving things you can't name.
  Grieving a timeline you never got to live in.
    Grieving the version of yourself who could have felt safe.
      Grieving all the friends you've lost to apathy.
        Grieving the joy that feels like a foreign language you once knew, but forgot somewhere between your first climate anxiety and your last emergency drill.

And the great betrayal is that this grief isn't publicly acknowledged. There are no communal rituals. No societal acknowledgments. Just wellness influencers saying "just stay positive" and politicians promising jobs on a planet whose soil is eroding beneath us. Grief, when unrecognized, becomes shame.

And when that shame lodges in you long enough, it becomes the belief that something is wrong with you.

But what if nothing's wrong with you?
What if everything is wrong with the world and your grief is your proof of still being intact?
Of still having a heart worth trusting?

Let me say this clearly:

You are allowed to grieve a world that was never real.
You are allowed to grieve a future that never came.
You are allowed to grieve for the person you were becoming before collapse interrupted.
You are allowed to grieve without explanation, without permission, without needing to turn it into a post, or a cause, or a creative project.

Your grief is enough.
And it is *sacred.*
And it is *useful.*

Not in the capitalist sense of productivity. But in the sense that grief clears space. It breaks the illusion. It makes room for what's next. It cracks the carapace of disillusionment so something alive can emerge from underneath.

Because the world is not going back.
But you don't have to go numb to survive it.
You can grieve—and in doing so, you create space for the *next story.*

The story that begins when we stop pretending everything's fine.
The story that begins with a sob, a whisper, a question.

The story that begins here.
With you.
Still feeling.
Still human.
Still holding the thread.

Even when the world forgets what it was weaving for.

Practice

The Grief Inventory

Make a list:

> *"Things I've lost (that no one saw)."*

Take your time.

Then write:

> *"Things I still carry (even when I don't want to)."*

Then this:

> *"Things I'm ready to lay down."*

This is not about fixing it.
This is about facing it.

And in that act,
you are already remaking the world.

VI.

IMAGINE LIKE LE GUIN

Or: The future is not a destination. It is a remembering.

CODE VIOLET

This chapter opens new worlds.

Let the future come sideways.

CO-REGULATION INVITATION

Doodle. Daydream.

Open a window and watch the clouds pass.

Fractal Nineteen

The Myth of the Given Future

They told you the future was a known destination
With likely waypoints: *college, career, family, retirement.*

That it was a timeline—a conveyor belt moving forward.
That your job was to find your spot on it,
Pick a career, pay your dues, do your part.
The tracks were already laid.
Your job was to ride.

But here's the truth:
That future was never real.
It was a story.

And if the story no longer serves,
you can write another one.[20]

---

[20] **Actual quote from Ursula K. Le Guin (2014):**
  "*We live in capitalism. Its power seems inescapable.
  So did the divine right of kings.*"

Fractal Twenty

Futures Are Grown, Not Predicted

You've been taught to ask:

>*What will the future look like?*

But the better question is:

>*What kind of future is worth growing?*

The future isn't a weather report.

It's not a spreadsheet.

It's not a simulation spit out by ChatGPT 18.3.4.

The future is a garden.[21]

And what you plant in it—your dreams, your doubts, your care, your anger—*matters.*

Especially now.

---

[21] **Inscribed on the back cover of a worn permaculture design workbook:** "*They will tell you there is no alternative. That's when you must begin to imagine harder.*"

Fractal Twenty-One

Solarpunk Is Not Sci-Fi
It's a Sense Memory

You already know what a better world feels like.

It smells like bread baking in a communal oven.

It sounds like a circle of kids laughing under solar lanterns.

It tastes like clean water that was never privatized.

It moves like a bike on a traffic-free street.

It rests like a nervous system that knows safety.

These are not fantasies.
These are *clues.*[22]
They live inside you.
They live in the land.
They live in the memory of what never was,
and still might be.

---

[22] **Sewn into a patch on the back of a protest jacket:**
"*Hope is not wishful thinking. It is a practice. A muscle. A map.*"

Fractal Twenty-Two

Dreaming Is an Act of Resistance

To imagine in the face of collapse is a rebellion.

To hope with clarity is a kind of weapon.

To wonder is to remember that *we are not done yet.*[23]

Even now,

  Even here,

    You can:

Sketch blueprints for a library made of reclaimed materials.

Compose a treaty between generations not yet born.

Build a currency where value is measured
in meals, not money.

Speak out loud the stories that never got airtime
because they didn't fit the algorithm.

This is not *escapism.*

This is *design.*

This is *refusal.*

This is *ancestral technology* rebooted through your breath.

---

[23] **Carved into a city park bench in winter:**
  "Maybe the most punk thing is to imagine joy and infrastructure."

Imagine Like Le Guin

Or, How to Remember the Future Without Getting Trapped in a Panic Attack About the Present

Let's begin with the word future, which is not, as most educational posters or social media captions might suggest, a place you're "going" to. You are not boarding a linear time train to "The Future™" where everyone wears biodegradable jumpsuits and speaks in a soft, inclusive tech dialect while sipping recycled rainwater matcha lattes and doing conflict resolution with neuro-sync devices. There is no train. There are no tracks. There is no ETA. And yet—and this is crucial—there is a future. But not in the singular, not in the way you were taught. Not as a forecast. Not as a payoff. The future is not a singular noun. It's a *field*.

The future is a plural. Futures, really. A wild proliferation. A garden of possibilities growing in every direction like kudzu or coral or speculative fiction. And if this makes you anxious, if your throat tightens every time someone says *"the next generation"* or *"by 2050,"* that's not because you're apathetic. That's because you know—on some soul level usually reserved for myths and breakups and late-night text messages you'll regret in the morning—that the futures being offered to you are *profoundly insufficient.*

Because what are your options, really?

> **Dystopia**, marketed as realism. *The future as ruin porn.*
> Endless Netflix specials and thinkpieces about what
> happens after the water runs out, after democracy
> collapses, after robots replace all the jobs and we're all
> living in bunkers eating cricket protein and livestreaming
> our loneliness for likes.

> **Utopia**, marketed as delusion. A greenwashed fantasy
> where everything's fixed by 2035 thanks to carbon credits
> and AI governance and some new billionaire-funded
> vertical farm in Dubai. A future that feels like someone
> else's Instagram: highly aesthetic, deeply alienating,
> suspiciously absent of mess.

> **Stasis**, marketed as normal. Just keep doing what you're
> doing. Maybe vote. Maybe recycle. Definitely download the
> mindfulness app. The world will keep spinning. Things
> aren't that bad.

Except: they are.
And you *know* it.
You can feel it, even when you can't explain it.
Especially then.

And so here's the dilemma: how do you imagine something better when every direction feels like a lie, or a trap, or just another version of the same story told in different fonts?

The answer, if there is one (and let's be honest, answers are rare and slippery things), isn't about *"thinking positive"* or *"manifesting"* or visualizing a better life until the algorithm delivers it. The answer begins with *remembering*.

Not remembering the past.
Remembering the future.

Which sounds impossible. Which sounds like poetry. Which is poetry. But also: it's neuroscience. It's history. It's a practice. It's what Ursula K. Le Guin knew, and why we invoke her now like a spell. Because Le Guin didn't write sci-fi to predict what would happen. She wrote it to show what could happen if we unshackled our imaginations from the empire of inevitability.

She reminded us that the real dystopia isn't collapse.
It's the inability to imagine anything else.

So here's a practice, maybe even a prayer:
You take a breath.
You look around at the wreckage—climate, capitalism, trust, your social battery.
And you say, quietly, without irony:
There is still a world worth building.

Not a perfect world. Not a clean world. Not a brand-safe world.

A world with compost. With arguments. With slow apologies.

A world with laughter that isn't monetized.

A world with time.

Time to heal.

Time to listen.

Time to build something durable in the ruins.

And you ask yourself:

> *What does water taste like when it isn't poisoned or bought? What does a day feel like when it doesn't revolve around extraction? What kind of education teaches you to belong—not just to succeed? What would it mean to have a nervous system that knows rest?*

You don't have to know the answers.

You just have to ask better questions.

You just have to imagine as if your imagination is real.
Because it is.

And this is the part that gets me, every time: the truth is, we've already tasted these futures. Not in full. Not at scale. But in flashes. In street kitchens after protests. In reclaimed lots turned into gardens. In queer houses where rent is shared and so are the dreams. In every act of mutual aid, unsponsored joy, and imperfect, persistent hope.

Those are not fantasies.
They are previews.

The future doesn't arrive all at once. It leaks in.
Through art. Through kinship. Through stubborn seeds.
Through you.

Yes, you.

With your cracked phone and climate grief and trauma-survival humor.
You, who still makes playlists for people you love.
You, who still cries at animated movies and wonders if that counts as softness.
You, who feels like maybe, possibly, you were born to help midwife something better.

You don't need a five-year plan.
You need a myth to live by.
A story that holds your grief and your gifts.
A world big enough to belong to.

Le Guin knew this. She didn't write futures as escape hatches.
She wrote them as remembering devices.

As portals to what we already know,

somewhere beneath the noise.

So:

You breathe.

You write.

You rage.

You imagine.

You remember.

And the future remembers you back.

Practice

The Remembered Future

Find a page.

  Or a window.

    Or a patch of dirt.

Now ask:

"What does safety smell like?"

"What does justice taste like?"

"What does community feel like in the body?"

Write it.

  Draw it.

    Name it.

      Tell someone.

You are not just imagining a new world.

You are remembering a forgotten one.

And that memory might just be the seed.

VII.
WE ORGANIZE
OR WE DRIFT

Or: How to build something better with people

who are also falling apart.

CODE YELLOW

This chapter draws a map.

You don't have to walk it alone.

CO-REGULATION INVITATION

Write down three people you trust.

Make a tiny list.

Light a candle.

Fractal Twenty-Three

Together Is the Only Way Through

There's a lie stitched into your timeline:

that you have to do this alone.

Alone in your room.

Alone in your grief.

Alone in your rage.

Alone trying to fix the world between class and curfew.

But loneliness is not nature.

  It's *design.*

And the antidote isn't bootstraps.

  It's *belonging.*

We survive by linking arms.[24]

We thrive by building systems that hold more than one person at

a time.

We organize.

Or we drift.

---

[24] **Scrawled on the ceiling of a shelter bunk bed:**
"The creative adult is the child who survived—and found others."

Fractal Twenty-Four

The Myth of the Solo Hero

The movies taught you wrong.

It's not one person with a sword or a prophecy.

It's not a lone genius with the answer.

The real revolution looks like:

      Group chats with purpose.

      Circles of consent.

      Delegated tasks.

      Shared snacks.

      Deep listening.

      Conflict that doesn't end in exile.

      Joy that isn't co-opted by branding.

The real hero is the team[25]

that doesn't fall apart

when the first plan fails.

---

[25] **Written in Sharpie on a student debt notice:**
"They will sell you individual freedom to distract you from collective power."

Fractal Twenty-Five
Mutual Aid Is Not Charity

Helping each other is not a luxury.

It's not "nice."

It's not a post-apocalyptic side quest.

It is *infrastructure.*

It is *medicine.*

It is *strategy.*

When the system breaks (again),

mutual aid is what fills the cracks.

Food shares.

Rides to clinics.

Housing swaps.

Class notes.

Breakup care packages.

Everything they forgot to teach us,

we remember together.[26]

---

[26] **Pooled in the page margins of a love letter never sent:**
"We are wired for connection. The systems aren't."

Fractal Twenty-Six

Start Small, Think Deep, Go Together

You don't have to start a movement.

You can:

> *Ask your friends what they're scared about.*
>
> *Host a listening circle.*
>
> *Map who's in your "we."*
>
> *Cook something.*
>
> *Share what you have.*
>
> *Repair what's broken.*
>
> *Learn how to disagree without ghosting.*
>
> *Make a decision with others—and trust the process.*

You don't have to be perfect.

You don't have to be the loudest.

You don't have to know all the acronyms.

Just don't drift alone.

Pull someone closer.[27]

Get in the same boat.

Row.

---

[27] **Found taped to a cracked mirror next to breathwork instructions:**
"Turns out the opposite of collapse isn't control. It's co-regulation."

We Organize or We Drift

Or, The Agonizing Miracle of Trying to Build a Better World With Other Human Beings Who Are Also Sleep-Deprived, Grief-Flooded, Chronically Overcommitted, and Still Somehow Hopeful

Let's begin with the obvious, because that's the thing that always gets skipped: *doing things alone is easier.*
Not better. Not wiser. Not more sustainable.
Just easier.
Less variables. Less personalities. Less email threads.
Less feelings.
You control the playlist. You do the work. You get the credit. You implode in private. Simple.

You've probably tried it. I certainly have. It goes something like this: you notice that the world is a burning simulation of itself—economically rigged, ecologically unraveling, spiritually bankrupt—and instead of screaming into the void (*which is also valid, by the way*), you decide to do something. You start a project. A movement. A zine. A Discord server. A weekly newsletter. A spontaneous revolution disguised as a student club. You make posters. You make rules. You make spreadsheets. You maybe get one or two other friends involved who nod enthusiastically but immediately ghost the moment things require a quorum.

Then the burnout hits. Or the groupchat turns radioactive. Or you realize you're somehow organizing a climate strike and managing everyone's interpersonal wounds and trying to graduate while not crumbling under the low hum of despair that lives under everything. So you quit. Or drift. Or delete the folder and convince yourself it didn't matter anyway.

Spoiler: it did.

Even if it failed.
Even if it fizzled.
Even if the mutual aid network you tried to start turned into a mutual ghosting network.
Because here's what no one told you—probably on purpose:
the work of liberation is deeply unglamorous.

It's not a montage.
  It's not a TED Talk.
    It's not a brand.

It's a long, messy, repetitive, relational, often silent slog through the weeds of human behavior. It's *infrastructure*, not inspiration. It's group process. It's conflict resolution that feels like emotional exfoliation. It's realizing someone you deeply admire is also deeply annoying in meetings. It's understanding that movements are made out of people, and people are made out of contradictions.

And yet.

There is nothing more holy, more defiant, more radically tender than organizing.

Not organizing like *"making flyers"* (though blessed be the
flyer-makers),
but organizing as in:

> We choose to belong to each other even when it's hard.

> We choose to build something real—even if it breaks and
> we try again.

> We choose to stay in the room, at the table, in the
> thread—because the alternative is drifting into isolated
> despair while the worst people consolidate more power
> with fewer ideas and better fonts.

The real revolution isn't aesthetic.
It's not slick. It's not meme-optimized.

It's sitting in a circle while someone cries about how the
decision-making process reminds them of their dad.
It's deciding whether to use Google Docs or Notion and realizing
this is actually a *values* conversation.
It's someone showing up late with snacks.
It's making a budget and realizing no one knows how to do math.
It's fixing that one person's pronouns on the flyer before printing
200 copies.
It's learning what consensus actually means—not theoretically,
but somatically—when you have to wait for that one person to
talk it through again because they just had a breakthrough.

And the work is slow. Which feels like failure, because we were
raised on plotlines where things change in thirty minutes or three
acts. But building takes time. Trust takes time. And if you're

paying attention, you're already late—but if you're building with care, you're right on time.

And yes, there will be drama.
There will be micro-disasters.
There will be spreadsheets with ten color-coded columns and someone will still ask *"what's the link?"* five seconds before the Zoom meeting starts.

But also:
There will be new friendships forged in fire.
There will be laughter so uncontrollable you'll forget why you were sad.
There will be moments where someone says, *"I've never felt this seen before,"* and you realize, in your body, that something just healed.
There will be food passed around, secrets shared, music played, memes created, and futures imagined that no longer feel like fiction.

There will be something *real.*

And this—this is why we organize.
Not because it's efficient.
But because it's the only way we stay human in a system that profits from our disconnection.

So yes, it's easier to drift.
To let the tide take you.
To pretend "someone else will handle it."
To believe you're too broken to help.

But drifting is not rest. Drifting is forgetting.

And if there's one thing I know (and it's not much, but this I trust):
the act of organizing is the act of remembering.
Remembering that we are not alone.
That we never were.
That the future is not something we wait for—*it's something we
make,* in messy kitchens and crowded living rooms and
underfunded libraries and late-night calls and last-minute
planning sessions where someone finally says:

> *"Wait...what if we just tried it this way?"*

And the world tilts.
  A little.
   Toward life.

Practice

The Circle Map

On a blank page, draw a small circle. That's you.

Around it, draw other circles.

> *Who's close to you?*
>
> *Who would you call at 3am?*
>
> *Who do you share memes with?*
>
> *Who can you build with?*

Now ask:

> *What do we need?*
>
> *What do we know?*
>
> *What can we offer?*

This is your circle of care.

Your crew.

Your council.

Your revolution.

Build from there.

VIII.
YOU ARE NOT A BRAND, YOU ARE A BEING

Or: The quiet art of unbecoming what the world demanded and remembering who you've always been.

CODE TEAL

This chapter dissolves illusions.

There's nothing wrong with being real.

CO-REGULATION INVITATION

Turn off your screens.

Touch something real—tree bark, skin, soil.

Remember your body.

Fractal Twenty-Seven
The Lie of the Feed

Somewhere along the way,

you were taught to curate yourself.

To post instead of exist.

To optimize instead of feel.

To brand instead of be.[28]

You became

a page,

a profile,

an aesthetic,

a pitch deck of a person.

You started asking not "Is *this me?*"

but wondering "*Will it get likes?*"

You are not alone.

But you are not a brand.

---

[28] **Lipsticked on a bathroom stall door:**
"*Perfectionism is a shield. Authenticity is a practice.*"

Fractal Twenty-Eight
Capitalism Wants You Confused

Let's be clear:

Capitalism wants your identity confused with your output.

It wants you to:

    Monetize your hobbies.

    Flatten your feelings into content.

    Hustle healing into a product.

    Turn your body into a storefront.

It wants you to mistake *visibility* for safety,
and *attention* for love.[29]

But you are not here to be consumed.
You are here to be *met*.

---

[29] **Scribbled in eyeliner over a canceled ad:**
"*The market will sell your face back to you. Don't let it sell your worth.*"

Fractal Twenty-Nine

The Performance is Exhausting

The endless self-editing.

The algorithmic smiling.

The pressure to have a "*take*," a "*thing*," a "*niche*."

To always be on-brand[30],

on-message,

on-camera.

Even when you're falling apart.

Even when your nervous system is screaming:

    rest.   *retreat.*   *reset.*

Even when your soul wants to go offline and

 just be

  weird

   quiet

    fluid

     free.

---

[30] **Carried forward from the Tao and Le Guin, softly penciled:**
"The name that can be spoken is not the true name."

Fractal Thirty

You Are Not an Algorithmic Artifact

You are not content.

You are not a product.

You are not a line item in someone else's attention economy.

You are a *being*.[31]

With breath.

With pulse.

With tears that matter even when no one is watching.

You are allowed to:

> *Change.*

> *Hide.*

> *Speak slowly.*

> *Be unremarkable.*

> *Exist without output.*

> *Be loved outside of performance.*

---

[31] **Typed in Courier font, low-contrast, never submitted:**
"The most radical thing you can do is nothing at all...and still be enough."

You Are Not a Brand, You Are a Being

Or, The Acute Discomfort of Trying to Remain a Whole Human Person in a Culture That's Asking You to Be a Marketable Slideshow With Good Lighting and Clear Value Propositions

There's a particular kind of fatigue that arises not from lack of sleep or caloric deficit or even mental overload in the classic sense, but from the ambient pressure of having to translate your entire being into something that makes sense to strangers in 1.8 seconds or less.

It's the tiredness of being interpretable.

And not in the generous, connective sense of interpretation—like someone reading a poem and seeing something in it that you never consciously meant but are nevertheless touched by—but in the economic sense, the commodified sense, the social-performance sense. The sense in which your face, your voice, your self-description, your tastes, your trauma history, your vibe, your font choices, your rate of dopamine-regulated emoji usage, your curated digital footprint, your "energy," your politics, your humor, and even your sadness—especially your sadness—are all under constant assessment. Not necessarily by anyone in particular. But by everyone in general. All the time. Through the feed.

And maybe you don't even feel it all at once. Maybe it just lives in your shoulders. In the way you click "backspace" six times before hitting "send." In the way you open TikTok not because you want to but because you have to. Because if you don't "show up," you disappear. And if you disappear, you stop existing. Not literally, obviously. But figuratively. Socially. Algorithmically. And what is a person in 2025 if not a node in other people's notifications?

There's no need to get mystical or even particularly moralistic about this. Let's just say plainly that when you are raised in an attention economy, you learn—consciously or not—to become *legible.*

You learn to smooth the weird edges, compress your contradictions, stylize your pain, weaponize your charm, rehearse authenticity, and package your story in a way that signals value to the network. Not because you're shallow. But because that's what survival looks like now. Because invisibility, in the era of perpetual display, is not neutrality—it's irrelevance. And irrelevance feels like death.

What this means, practically speaking, is that being a "good person" becomes indistinguishable from being a *compelling narrative object.* One who is educational, self-aware, emotionally fluent, anti-oppressive, trauma-informed, mentally ill but not too mentally ill, capable of being sad in digestible doses, and always, always on-message.

So the "self" becomes a campaign.
The campaign becomes the brand.
And the brand becomes the self.

And maybe you're reading this thinking, "Okay, but I don't even post that much. I'm not an influencer. I mostly lurk." Which is fair. But the performative gaze doesn't require you to post—it just requires you to *think in terms of posting.* It requires your interiority to imagine itself being watched, scanned, rated, misread. It requires you to be fluent in the gestures of relatability, to perform closeness as a strategy, to aestheticize pain as preemptive control. Even when you're silent. Especially when you're silent.

None of this is your fault.
But it is happening inside of you.

And maybe you're starting to notice that it doesn't feel good.

That even your joy feels overlit.
That even your privacy feels constructed.
That even your reflection has started talking back to you in Canva templates.

And you're tired.

Not existentially tired in the way of the classics—Camusian, Kafkaesque, the whole "what is the meaning of life" circuit—but admin tired. Identity admin. Emotional admin. A constant low-level spreadsheet of self-calibration. Which version of me do they want today? Which caption makes me seem okay-but-not-too-okay? How do I look interesting without trying to look like I'm trying?

You start to long for something unshaped.
Not in a regressive or anti-tech or

let's-move-to-a-cabin-and-never-use-phones-again way. Just...
unmediated.
Just... allowed to exist without being useful.

Which is hard. Because the opposite of branding is not "bad
branding."
It's being. And being doesn't convert well.

Being is boring.
Being is slow.
Being is unoptimized.
Being is you in your room, lying on the floor, not knowing what to
do next.
Being is messy laughter with no captions.
Being is a conversation that doesn't lead to a conclusion.
Being is trusting that you are real even when no one is watching.

And in the world we're in—the one you didn't ask for but are
nevertheless inside of—being is also deeply, weirdly, threatening.
Because if you're not selling something (even just a version of
yourself), then how does the system know what to do with you?

The truth is: it doesn't.

And that's the point.

Because you're not a commodity.
You're not a project.
You're not a timeline.

You're a person.

Which is not a brandable thing.
Which is the whole miracle.

So if you're tired, you're not failing.
If you're confused, you're not broken.
If you're overwhelmed, you're not alone.
You're just a person in a system that wants you to forget that
being a person is already enough.

There's no clever ending to this. No five-point action plan for
reclaiming your identity in the age of synthetic selves. There's just
a small invitation. A pause.

To close the tab.
To go outside.
To forget the script.
To eat a piece of fruit slowly.
To laugh badly.
To feel something you don't have words for yet.

To exist, just for a minute,
without having to make it make sense.

Practice

The De-Branding Ritual

Tonight—or whenever the scroll feels heavier than your heart— log off.

Write on a piece of paper:

> *"I am not a brand. I am a being."*

Then write:

> *What am I without the likes?*
>
> *What parts of me exist when no one's looking?*
>
> *Who am I becoming when I stop performing?*

Put it under your pillow.
Let it haunt you gently.

You are not what you post.
You are not your likes.
You are not your follower count.

You are a becoming.
  Not a brand.

And you are enough.

IX.
SACRED FUTILITY AND EVERYDAY MAGIC

Or: Why we still bother to do the small beautiful things, even when they "won't change anything."

CODE BLUE

This chapter lives in the paradox.

Meaning doesn't always shout.

CO-REGULATION INVITATION

Water a plant.

Sweep a floor.

Do something small and

real without asking why.

Fractal Thirty-One

The World Is on Fire and You're Making Soup

It's Tuesday.

The sky is the wrong color.

The news feels like satire.

And you just spent 40 minutes making soup.[32]

From scratch.

You chopped onions like a monk.

You stirred as if someone was watching (they weren't).

You tasted. Adjusted. Shared.

And for a moment—

you forgot the doom.

Or maybe not forgot.

You just remembered something else, too.

Something warm.

Something alive.

Something worth returning to.

---

[32] **Written in the margin of a recipe book next to soup stains:**
"We can't do it all. But we can still do something. And sometimes that something is soup."

Fractal Thirty-Two

The Lie of Scale

The world wants you to think:

If it won't change everything, it doesn't matter.

If it won't fix the system.

If it won't go viral.

If it won't become legislation.

If it won't impress someone.

Then why bother?[33]

But that's not how life works.

That's not how healing works.

That's not how you work.

Small things are not less than.

They are the *root system*.

Invisible. Quiet. Absolutely essential.

---

[33] **Whispered through ritual smoke by someone whose name we never caught:**
"The true name of magic is attention."

Fractal Thirty-Three

Tiny Acts of Unreasonable Care

A text that says "Thinking of you."

A poem written but never posted.

Brushing your cat with both hands.

Watering the same sad houseplant for the sixth time.

Wiping down a table no one asked you to.

Lighting a candle at 2pm. For no reason.

These things do not scale.[34]

They do not optimize.

They *remind you:*

> You are not a machine.

> You are not a transaction.

> You are still capable of beauty
> even in the wreckage.

---

[34] **Scribbled on the inside flap of a banned book:**
"*When they can't extract value from your joy, they call it useless. That's how you know it's sacred.*"

Fractal Thirty-Four

The Point of the Pointless

You might wonder:

What's the point?

The answer might be:

It is the point.

The kiss on the forehead.
The doodle in the notebook.
The dance in the hallway.
The ten-minute walk with no destination.

These are not distractions.
These are *evidence*.[35]
That you are still here.
Still paying attention.
Still capable of loving something
that doesn't serve a purpose.

And that, maybe,
is the real purpose.

---

[35] **Found beside a coffee ring on a rejection letter:**
"*Weirdly, I think doing something kind and quiet when it won't be noticed is the only real proof we're alive.*"

Sacred Futility and Everyday Magic

Or, The Perplexing and Slightly Embarrassing Compulsion to Keep Doing Small, Pointless Things That No One Will Ever Applaud You For, and Why That Might Actually Be the Most Honest Response to Everything

There's a kind of fatigue that sets in after a certain amount of cumulative exposure to the news, or the internet, or people who talk with certainty about "systems change," where the basic premise of life itself begins to feel a little...fragile. Not fragile like eggshells or crystal, but fragile like a dream you can't quite remember the details of, only that you woke up sad. The fatigue isn't loud. It's not burnout in the classic sense. It's not even depressive, exactly. It's more like a spiritual buffering symbol.

You know what I'm talking about.

It's the moment when you open your phone and scroll through a series of increasingly surreal headlines (drought in the Amazon, fascism in the legislature, rent strike in your hometown, another extinction ticked off like a footnote) and then, somehow, you find yourself in the kitchen folding a dishtowel into thirds so that it sits just right on the oven handle.

This is not activism.

This is not a solution.

This is not even coping in any productive way.

But you do it.

And here's the thing. You do it again.

You stir the soup slowly.

You wipe the table twice.

You sit for ten extra seconds with your tea, for no good reason, just because it smells good.

This is the part I want to talk about. Because there's something here. Something small and stupid and sacred. Something that doesn't scale, doesn't sell, doesn't solve a single systemic problem and yet refuses to go away.

Let's just call it what it is: *pointless care.*

And it matters.

I want to be clear: this is not a defense of apathy, or detachment, or pretending things are okay when they're not. You are smart enough to know that the planet is not "going through a rough patch." You know that what we're facing is complex and compounding and accelerating. The climate isn't just changing—it's fraying. Inequality isn't just bad—it's structural and sticky and written into the software of everything. And yes, it's overwhelming. Of course it is. You'd have to be clinically dissociated—or extremely well-paid—not to be overwhelmed.

And yet.

You still made the soup.

You still tied your friend's shoelace when it came undone.
You still picked up the wrapper someone else dropped on the
sidewalk.
You still pet the cat.
You still hummed a song for no audience.
You still remembered someone's birthday, even though you forgot
your password and your deadlines and what hope is supposed to
feel like.

And I think there's something deeply true in that. Something the
big systems can't account for.

Because it's not resistance in the traditional sense.
 It's not even resilience, really.
 It's more like *unreasonable tenderness.*

A refusal to surrender your attention to despair.
 A quiet agreement with life that says: Yes, I see the wreckage. I
still choose to sweep this corner of the room.

This isn't magic. This isn't heroic. This isn't some grand spiritual
insight masquerading as a dish-drying ritual. This is *ordinary
behavior* that has, in a system built to extract and flatten and
reward only what can be measured, become quietly subversive.

Because to care—when no one is watching, when nothing
depends on it, when there is no reward—is to insist on being *a
person*, not a data point.

And I know. There's a danger here. That this kind of thinking becomes an excuse for inaction, for narcissistic detachment disguised as mindfulness. "At least I made the bed today," says the man whose neighborhood is on fire. But that's not what I mean. I'm not romanticizing the tiny thing as a replacement for the real thing. I'm just saying: sometimes, the tiny thing is real. And it doesn't need to prove itself to be worth doing.

This is not hope as in "things will get better."
This is not strategy as in "here's how we win."
This is something else. Something slower. Something quieter.

This is *staying inside your life*, even when the world makes no sense.

Not to fix it.
Not to flee it.
Just... to remain.

And so yes, the world is ending in some ways. But also: you brushed someone's hair out of their eyes. You remembered the name of the street where you first kissed someone. You gave someone your last clean fork because you knew they needed it more than you. You read a poem out loud, and for once, no one interrupted. You made a playlist that no one asked for. You whispered "good night" to the dark.

None of this changes the system.

And yet.
It does something.
To you.

To us.
To the air.

Which might be more than nothing.
Which might be the whole point.
Which might be the only thing left to do
  once we stop trying to win,
    and start trying to stay human.

Practice

The Useless Joy List

Write down three things you do that make no sense.

That no one rewards.

That no one sees.

That make you feel a little more like you.

Now do one.

On purpose.

With reverence.

Welcome to the Church of the Ordinary.

Welcome to the Revolution of Enough.

X.

ADD YOUR PAGE

Or: The book ends here, but the world doesn't.

CODE VIOLET

This chapter belongs to you.

Write what only you can say.

CO-REGULATION INVITATION

Play music.

Light incense.

Write without editing.

Share if it feels good.

Fractal Thirty-Five

This Was Never Just a Book

You've been reading.

Thinking.

Feeling.

Pausing.

Looping back.

Maybe scribbling notes in the margins.

Maybe copying one sentence onto your wall.

Maybe rolling your eyes at another.

But this was never just a book.

 It was a mirror.

A map.

A quiet hand on your shoulder.

A voice reminding you that you are not alone.

And now:

It's your turn.[36]

---

[36] **Whispered from the fold of a well-worn coat:**
 "The story is not finished when the book ends. The story begins when it's carried forward."

Fractal Thirty-Six

What Do You Know Now?

Not what you've memorized.

What you've felt.

What you've cracked open.

What you've unlearned.

Not facts.

But truths.

Not doctrine.

But experience.

What do you know about:

> *Grief*
> *Anger*
> *Friendship*
> *Futility*
> *Hope*
> *Attention*
> *Touch*
> *Belonging?*

What do you know now that you didn't before?[37]

Write it.

Whisper it.

Pass it on.

---

[37] **Jotted on the back of a bus ticket that is still valid for another hour:** *"Every page is a permission slip. This one's yours."*

Fractal Thirty-Seven

There Is No Perfect Ending

The temptation is to make it neat.

Tie a bow.

Summarize the message.

Land the plane.

But you know better now.

Nothing real ends neatly.[38]

It continues.

It echoes.

It composts.

The question is not "What did you learn?"

It is:

"*What will you carry?*"

---

[38] **Crossed out and rewritten in the corner of a blank page:**
"Maybe the final chapter is the one you write without asking anyone's permission."

Fractal Thirty-Eight

This Is the Place You Begin

A blank page.

A pause.

A question mark.

A seed.

What if the next story is slower?

Softer?

More rooted?

More you?

Write one sentence.

Write ten.

Write none.

But know this:

>Your life is not the footnote.
>
>It's the next chapter.

And we are listening.

Add Your Page

Or, What Comes After the Last Chapter When There's Still Something Left in You That's Unsayable

There's this moment that happens near the end of most books—usually subtle, occasionally theatrical—where the author tries to deliver the "closing note," the resonant sentence or moral takeaway or grand epiphany that, ideally, wraps everything in a nice velvet cord of significance. Something that says: we've arrived. Something final.

And I think it's important to say, right here, that I don't have that.

Not because the preceding pages didn't matter. Not because the ideas didn't accumulate. But because the end of a book—especially a book like this, if we can even call it that—is a false thing. Or, if not false, then at least inherently incomplete. Because you're incomplete. And I am. And the world is. And that incompleteness is not a flaw in the design. It is the whole point. It's what lets us keep going.

You don't reach the end and suddenly become someone new. You reach the end and carry something with you. Maybe a sentence. Maybe a silence. Maybe just a kind of ache that doesn't have a shape yet but feels important.

And what you carry forward doesn't belong to me.
It belongs to you.
Which is why this section is here.

Not as a conclusion.
But as a handing-off.

There's a kind of humility, I think, in ending without closure. In resisting the urge to deliver a summation. To say, "This is what it means." To construct some tidy frame around what was never tidy to begin with.

Because whatever this was—this whole thing we just did together—it wasn't an argument. It wasn't a thesis. It wasn't a campaign for hope or a performance of despair. It was a long, strange, anxious, occasionally poetic, often spiraling attempt to name the condition of being alive right now with at least some fidelity to the weird, fractured texture of that experience.

And now that it's almost over, the most honest thing I can do is step aside.

Which doesn't mean disappearing. It just means **making room**. For your words. Your sketches. Your memories. Your own version of this experience, which is always already different from mine.

And look, maybe you don't feel ready. Maybe nothing came up for you while reading. Or maybe too much did, and you don't know where to start. That's okay. There's no assignment here. No prompt to complete. No expectation to fulfill. Just a page. Blank. Open. Waiting.

And yeah, the metaphor is obvious. But it's also true.

There's a page in front of you.
What do you want to put on it?

Not what do you think you should say.
Not what would make a good impression.
Not what would impress your inner critic or outer teacher or some imagined audience scanning for virtue or cleverness.

Just... what's there?

Even if it's dumb. Even if it's just a date.
Even if it's a list of things you forgot to do today.
Even if it's "I don't know what to write."

Because that's real.
And real is enough.

You've made it this far. You've carried this book in your hands or on your screen or inside your head, through whatever mess your life currently is. You've lingered in these paragraphs—maybe skimmed some, maybe reread others—and that means something. Even if I don't know what, even if you don't know what.

And maybe the best we can do with that uncertainty is to sit beside it. To mark it. To write it down.

So this isn't the ending. This is the part where I stop. And you continue.

And not because I'm instructing you to. Not because you have to. But because—whether you write something down or not—**you are already writing the next page.**

In the way you show up.
In the way you speak.

In the way you treat the people around you.
In the way you treat yourself.

That's the book now.
It's you.

So go ahead.
Say something.
Even if it's small.
Even if it's quiet.
Even if it's just a gesture toward meaning.

The page is yours.

Always was.

Practice

Your Page

Take a real page—at the back of this book, or somewhere nearby.

Add your truths.

Your sketches.

Your fragments.

Your map.

Your rage.

Your recipe.

Your one true sentence.

Date it.

Sign it.

Fold it up.

Give it to a friend.

Leave it in a library book.

Burn it on the solstice.

Read it out loud to a tree.

Make it yours.

Because you were never just reading this.

You were always **writing it, too.**

A **BRIEF** HISTORY OF THE POLY**CRISIS**

(*AS IT CONTINUES TO **UNFOLD**)

Waves of the Polycrisis
A Brief Historical Timeline

First Wave: Extraction and Empire

[1500s–1800s] *The dominant worldview was **dominion and hierarchy**. Nature was seen as inert — a resource to be exploited. Non-European peoples were classified as inferior — tools, obstacles, or curiosities. The Earth was no longer a living mother, but a warehouse of materials ordained for extraction. Philosophy and theology rationalized conquest: "civilizing missions," "manifest destiny," "terra nullius." The sacred was severed from the soil, and profit was crowned king.*

1492: Columbus lands in the Americas, initiating widespread Indigenous dispossession.

1500–1867: Transatlantic Slave Trade moves millions into forced labor.

1600s–1700s: Industrial-scale whaling, coal mining, sugar plantations reshape ecosystems.

1750–1800: Early spikes in atmospheric CO_2 (pre-industrial baseline breached).

Second Wave: Industrial Acceleration and Carbon Unleashing

*[c. 1850–1945] The dominant ethos was **progress through mastery**. Machines were worshipped; human will was believed capable of total control over nature. Social Darwinism twisted evolution into hierarchies of "winners" and "losers." Fossil fuels became the unseen gods beneath steel, steam, and smoke. Colonial conquest turned into industrial conquest; speed became synonymous with success.Efficiency was sanctified, and the deep rhythms of Earth were drowned out by the ticking of factory clocks.*

1760–1840: Industrial Revolution in Britain; spreads globally by late 1800s.

1859: First commercial oil well drilled (Titusville, Pennsylvania).

1886: First automobile (Benz Motorwagen) paves way for car-driven cities.

1914–1918: World War I industrialized global conflict.

1945: U.S. detonates first atomic bombs (*Hiroshima* and *Nagasaki*).

1945: Founding of the United Nations (attempt to regulate global conflict post-WWII)

Third Wave: The Great Acceleration

[1945–1970s] The post-war dream crowned **growth as salvation**. *GDP became the metric of health, not forests, not happiness, not kinship. A utopian faith in technology, capitalism, and scientific management spread — the "American Dream" on global export. The commons were privatized; abundance was measured in possessions. Environmental damage was externalized, invisible beyond the suburbs and television screens. Progress was framed as endless and inevitable — a future without consequence.*

1945–1970: Global population doubles; energy use quadruples.

1956: M. King Hubbert predicts peak U.S. oil production (Hubbert's Peak).

1958: Keeling Curve begins (direct CO_2 measurements at Mauna Loa Observatory).

1962: *Silent Spring* by Rachel Carson catalyzes environmental awareness.

1970: First Earth Day celebrated (April 22).

1972: Club of Rome publishes *Limits to Growth* report, an early warning on resource exhaustion.

Fourth Wave: Globalization and Fragmentation

[1980s–2008] *The gospel became* **markets know best.**
Neoliberalism enthroned individualism: freedom was redefined as consumer choice, not collective wellbeing. Deregulation unleashed finance; public goods were eroded in favor of private profit. Ecological warnings were softened into marketing slogans: "green capitalism," "sustainable growth." Global inequality widened while the illusion of opportunity was maintained through branding and screens. The sacred was now a commodity; belonging was replaced with branding.

1979: Margaret Thatcher elected Prime Minister of the UK; neoliberalism ascends.

1980: Ronald Reagan elected U.S. President; deregulation policies expand.

1985: Ozone hole discovered over Antarctica.

1988: IPCC established to assess climate change risks.

1989–1991: Fall of Berlin Wall, collapse of Soviet Union "end of history" myth declared.

1994: NAFTA signed — accelerates global trade deregulation.

1997: Kyoto Protocol adopted, the first major global climate treaty (later undermined).

1999: Seattle WTO Protests ("Battle of Seattle") — Global resistance to corporate-led globalization explodes into public consciousness. Activists warn of labor exploitation, environmental destruction, and corporate overreach.

1999–2001: Dot-com Bubble Burst — Massive speculative collapse in tech sector reveals fragility of new digital economy. Sets stage for later financialization excesses.

2000: Human Genome Project Draft Completed — Biotechnology revolution promises to "reprogram life" itself, raising profound ethical and systemic risks around corporate biopower.

2001: 9/11 Terrorist Attacks — September 11, 2001: global shock event. Launches War on Terror, expanding surveillance states, militarized economies, political destabilization worldwide.

2001–2003: Invasions of Afghanistan and Iraq — Costly, destabilizing wars erode U.S. global legitimacy and destabilize the Middle East permanently.

2002: Enron and WorldCom Collapses — Early corporate financial scandals reveal deep rot inside deregulated capitalism (foreshadowing 2008 crash).

2004: Indian Ocean Tsunami — One of the deadliest natural disasters in modern history (230,000+ deaths), highlighting vulnerability of coastal populations and disaster response gaps.

2005: Hurricane Katrina — Climate disaster and racialized government failure in the U.S.; sharpens awareness of disaster capitalism and environmental injustice.

2006: Stern Review on the Economics of Climate Change — Major report warning that climate inaction will cost far more than prevention — largely ignored politically.

2007: Global Food Crisis Begins — Rising oil prices, biofuel production, and financial speculation cause food prices to spike, leading to hunger and political unrest in dozens of countries.

2007: iPhone Launches — Smartphones revolutionize human connectivity, attention economies, and social dynamics; new vulnerabilities emerge (algorithmic manipulation, dopamine-driven surveillance capitalism).

2007: IPCC Fourth Assessment Report — Confirms human-driven climate change with high confidence, warning of accelerating risks.

September 15, 2008: Lehman Brothers collapses, triggering global financial meltdown.

2008: U.S. Green Jobs Act gains momentum — Localized *"green collar"* movements begin focusing on environmental justice and economic opportunity (Van Jones, *The Green Collar Economy*).

2008–2012: Global recession deepens inequality and political instability.

Fifth Wave:
Compounding Shocks and Systemic Unraveling

If the **Fourth Wave** was the age of **markets over meaning**—*where neoliberalism fragmented the commons and repackaged alienation as freedom*—then the **Fifth Wave** *is what happens when the externalized costs of that system come back to collect. Between 2008 and 2025, a series of interlocking shocks reshaped the planet—not as isolated events, but as cascading failures within an already strained system. Finance. Climate. Health. Democracy. Trust. They didn't just falter.*

They fed one another.
In this period, collapse ceased to be a singular outcome.
It became the condition we were asked to normalize.

And yet, amid the disorientation, something else emerged: a growing refusal. Resistance no longer looked like protest alone—it looked like networks, co-ops, rematriation, youth tribunals, and underground care webs. It looked like people choosing each other over systems that had chosen profit.

This section traces six major shockwaves—not as a complete record, but as seismic pulses that reshaped the foundations of the present.

Shockwave I – The Initial Crack (2008–2012)
Shockwave II – Rising Resistance (2013–2016)
Shockwave III – Reckoning and Reaction (2017–2019)
Shockwave IV – Pandemic Polycrisis (2020–2021)
Shockwave V – Breach of Boundaries (2022–2023)
Shockwave VI – Feedback Loop Era (2024–2025)

Shockwave I: The Initial Crack (2008–2012)

"Collapse" doesn't usually look like fire and brimstone. It looks like a bank run. A job lost. A neighborhood gutted. It looks like being told "the worst is over" when it very much is not.

In 2008, Lehman Brothers imploded and took much of the global economy with it. The event wasn't the beginning of the unraveling, but it was the moment millions of people realized the house was already full of termites—and the inspectors were in on the scam.

Governments raced to bail out the banks with public money, spinning it as necessary to "save the system." But the system they saved was the one that broke us: a casino economy of derivatives and debt, built on decades of deregulation and trickle-down myths.

Meanwhile, everyday people were left to drown quietly in paperwork: foreclosure notices, unemployment claims, bankruptcy filings. The streets stayed quiet—at first.

Timeline Snapshots THE LITANY

2008: Global financial crash detonates following the collapse of Lehman Brothers; $10 trillion in global wealth evaporates in weeks.

2009: 350.org launches, led by Bill McKibben and youth activists—framing the climate crisis in clear planetary thresholds (350 ppm).

2010: The Deepwater Horizon spill pours over 200 million gallons of oil into the Gulf of Mexico. Government response is slow, corporate accountability slower.

2010–2012: The Arab Spring ignites across North Africa and the Middle East, catalyzed by food insecurity, corruption, and despair.

2011: Occupy Wall Street begins in Zuccotti Park. The 99% have found their voice—but not yet their power.

2011: Idle No More emerges in Canada—an Indigenous-led movement reclaiming land, language, and law from colonial erasure.

Deeper Forces SYSTEMIC LAYER

If the news cycle made it feel like a string of "bad years," the underlying currents were much deeper:

The *financial system* had decoupled from human need. It no longer served the public—it extracted from it.

The *climate system* was warning us, clearly and repeatedly—but emissions kept rising.

The *media system* was fracturing. Social media platforms began to replace traditional journalism with algorithmic frenzy. Truth itself began to splinter.

The *political system* defaulted to austerity: punish the poor to protect the market.

Cultural Fracture WORLDVIEW LAYER

The myth of inevitable progress—of markets as benevolent, of science as savior, of democracy as destiny—began to flicker. It wasn't dead, but it was gasping.

Even those who had "done everything right"—gone to school, bought homes, worked hard—found themselves precarious. Trust in institutions started leaking like oil from a busted pipe.

"The system isn't broken," someone in the crowd at Occupy muttered. "It's functioning exactly as designed."

Glimmers of Otherwise MYTHIC LAYER

And yet. Even amidst the wreckage, something stirred.

*Arab youth took to the streets not just in protest,
but in choreography—a dance of democracy rising.*

*In Louisiana, after the oil spill, communities
gathered not to mourn only, but to plan.*

*At Zuccotti Park, people cooked together, argued, shared skills,
raised tents, passed mics. For a brief, flickering moment, another way of
being glimmered into view: not profit, but presence.
Not efficiency, but care.*

*This wasn't a revolution. Not yet. It was a rupture.
A tear in the veil of inevitability.*

And once torn, it stayed torn.

Shockwave II: Rising Resistance (2013–2016)

There's a point—psychologically, politically—when you stop asking "Is this normal?" And instead ask, "Who benefits from this being normal?"

By the mid-2010s, the shocks of the Fifth Wave weren't just happening to people—they were being metabolized *by* them. A generation raised amid collapse was coming of age, and they weren't buying the story that history was over or that change only came through polite channels.

This was the age of sacred refusal. Of feet in the soil and code in the cloud. Of decentralized uprisings with no single leader, no unified demands—and no off switch.

Timeline Snapshots ^{THE LITANY}

2013: Greta Thunberg's solitary school strikes begin to seed *Fridays for Future.*

2014: *People's Climate March* draws 400,000+ to NYC—labor, faith, Indigenous, and climate justice movements show up side by side.

2015: The *Paris Agreement* is signed. Ambitious in symbolism, insufficient in substance.

2015–2016: *Standing Rock* resistance ignites—Sioux and allies oppose the Dakota Access Pipeline, echoing through global movements ("*Mni Wiconi* – Water is Life").

2016: *Brexit* passes; *Trump* is elected. The populist wave breaks through the center.

2016: #NoDAPL camps swell to historic size—largest Indigenous-led environmental resistance in modern U.S. history.

2016: *Extinction Rebellion* launches in the UK, demanding radical climate action through mass nonviolent disruption.

Structural Shifts <small>SYSTEMIC LAYER</small>

While mainstream narratives were still touting "post-recession recovery," lived experience told another story:

Inequality had deepened, not shrunk. The top 1% didn't just rebound—they soared.

Climate agreements gave the illusion of coordination while emissions continued rising.

Police militarization and surveillance metastasized in the name of "security."

Indigenous and youth movements emerged as moral leaders—less because of their novelty, more because institutions had lost moral authority.

The resistance wasn't just about carbon. It was about sovereignty. About dignity. About *whose future was being sacrificed* to keep the machine running.

Belief Cracks <small>WORLDVIEW LAYER</small>

By now, it was hard to believe the grown-ups had it under control. The center was not holding—it was being held up by branding, bureaucracy, and delay.

Two worldviews collided:

1. Progress is inevitable; trust the institutions.
2. Progress has been a lie for most of us; build from the ground.

The first was still dominant in the media, the schools, the policies. The second was spreading through hashtags, hand-painted banners, sacred fires, and circle meetings under tarps.

"What if hope isn't something you have, but something you do?"

Emergent Alternatives ^{MYTHIC LAYER}

The idea that we could *grow our way out of collapse* was beginning to rot. In its place: relational resurgence.

Land was not just land. *It was ancestor. It was* **teacher.**
Protest was not just disruption. *It was ceremony.* **Reclamation.**
Justice was not abstract. *It was water, breath, kin,* **sovereignty**.

The resistance camps—at Standing Rock, across Europe, in Hong Kong and Ferguson and São Paulo—weren't utopias. But they were laboratories. They tested a different myth: *that community, not capital, was the true infrastructure of survival.*

And they asked a brutal question, one that continues to echo:

> *If the system itself is producing crisis,*
> *what exactly are we trying to fix?*

Shockwave III: Reckoning and Reaction (2017–2019)

By 2017, the veil was off. The world wasn't trending toward equilibrium—it was teetering. Fires were getting bigger. Storms were getting weirder. Politics were getting nastier. And amidst it all, kids were walking out of school and saying what most adults wouldn't: *You lied to us about the future.*

The story of these years isn't just about heat—it's about friction. Between generations. Between realities. Between systems on autopilot and movements trying to pull the brake.

Timeline Snapshots THE LITANY

2017: *Women's March* becomes the largest single-day protest in U.S. history. Intersectional feminism hits the streets.

2017: *Sunrise Movement* launches—youth organizing for a Green New Deal with moral clarity and bold political demands.

2018: IPCC Special Report on 1.5°C warns that even "safe" warming targets will bring catastrophic consequences.

2018: *Fridays for Future* explodes—Greta Thunberg's solitary protest becomes millions strong.

2018: The *Red Deal* is proposed by Indigenous thinkers—an unapologetically radical alternative to neoliberal "green" transitions.

2019: *Hong Kong protests* erupt in sustained, decentralized resistance to authoritarian expansion.

2019: *Amazon and Australian wildfires* dominate global headlines—lungs of the planet ablaze.

2019: *Land Back* campaigns gain ground, reframing environmental justice as decolonization.

Underlying Currents SYSTEMIC LAYER

This wasn't just more bad news. It was an *acceleration*—a quickening of contradictions.

Democratic systems were failing to respond to climate science at scale.

Corporate climate pledges proliferated, but emissions kept rising—greenwashing became a core PR strategy.

The media ecosystem rewarded outrage and distraction, even as scientific warnings sharpened.

The youth uprising became the moral compass—mocked, minimized, yet persistent.

The data was undeniable. The timelines were tight. But meaningful institutional action remained elusive. Climate summits became rituals of delay disguised as diplomacy.

And in this vacuum, *something else* emerged.

Cultural Mood WORLDVIEW LAYER

Two emotional poles dominated public consciousness:

- *Grief*: the slow heartbreak of ecological awareness.
- *Defiance*: the refusal to surrender meaning or agency.

The myth of technocratic salvation began to lose coherence. So did the myth of endless economic growth. What replaced them wasn't a clean narrative—but a chaotic cacophony: doomscrolling, collapse memes, prepper culture, eco-anxiety, solarpunk dreams, climate denialism, all colliding in a digital agora.

The adults aren't going to save us.

And yet, that wasn't the end of the sentence.
The implied second half was always:

So we're going to save each other.

Emergent Alternatives Mythic Layer

Out of the wreckage, stories of *interdependence* started to reassert themselves. Not always loud. Not always coherent. But present.

Youth-led movements began forging direct links with Indigenous elders and land protectors.

Climate justice frameworks centered race, class, and geography—not just CO_2.

New symbols entered the lexicon: the hourglass, the fire emoji, the red handprint across the face, the upside-down flag.

Even the words shifted.

It wasn't just about "sustainability" anymore—it was about *survivability*. Not just about "climate change"—but about *climate justice, climate grief, climate rage.*

This was no longer a debate about the science. It was a battle over *story*—whose future mattered, and who got to define what counted as a solution.

Not everyone was preparing for the same apocalypse.
Some were preparing to adapt.
Others were preparing to profit.
And a few were preparing to transform.

Shockwave IV: Pandemic Polycrisis (2020–2021)

The virus didn't break the system.
It showed us the system was already broken.

If the 2010s were about sensing that something was off, 2020 was the year the floor gave way—and the whole world fell in together, unevenly.

A virus, invisible and indifferent, did what decades of climate science, anti-racist organizing, and economic critique could not: it made collapse *visible, simultaneous,* and *undeniably interconnected.*

It exposed which bodies were protected and which were expendable. It made clear that "normal" was a machine that had been running on injustice, and many didn't want to return to it.

Timeline Snapshots ^{THE LITANY}

March 11, 2020: WHO declares COVID-19 a global pandemic. Borders close. Cities lock down.

Spring 2020: Mutual aid networks proliferate—neighbors feed neighbors, organizers repurpose networks for survival.

May 25, 2020: George Floyd is murdered. Uprising ignites across the U.S. and beyond. *"I can't breathe"* becomes both a protest chant and a planetary condition.

2020: Oil prices briefly turn negative; entire sectors of the economy grind to a halt.

2020: Record-breaking hurricane season in the Atlantic. Wildfires devastate California and Australia.

January 6, 2021: U.S. Capitol insurrection—white rage on full display, democracy on the brink.

February 2021: Texas energy grid collapses during a cold snap. Deaths follow.

Summer–Fall 2021: Line 3 pipeline resistance intensifies. Indigenous water protectors lead mass mobilization.

August 2021: IPCC releases "Code Red for Humanity" report. Again, the alarm is sounded. Again, governments nod solemnly—and delay.

Deeper Mechanics SYSTEMIC LAYER

The pandemic didn't *cause* inequality, surveillance creep, or ecological fragility. It accelerated all three.

Supply chains buckled—exposing global dependencies built for efficiency, not resilience.

Essential workers were celebrated in hashtags, sacrificed in policy.

Public health systems, long underfunded, cracked under pressure.

Social media became both lifeline and toxin—spreading masks of care and clouds of misinformation.

The global response was split-screened: billionaires got richer, while billions struggled to breathe—literally and figuratively.

Capitalism adapted. Quickly. It always does. But what was growing beneath the surface wasn't just resistance—it was refusal.

Cultural Mood <small>WORLDVIEW LAYER</small>

The early lockdowns brought a strange silence. For a moment, dolphins returned to harbors (or so the meme claimed). Skies cleared. Birdsong grew audible.

People noticed things they hadn't noticed before:
The emptiness of commutes. The violence of normal.
The ache of disconnection. The hunger for care.

For some, it was a nervous breakdown.
For others, it was a spiritual reckoning.

We are not going back to normal because normal was the problem.

At the same time, the polarization intensified. Masks became battle flags. Vaccines became identity markers. Truth itself seemed to fragment further.

The information ecosystem, already teetering, became fully unmoored. Conspiracy met coping mechanism. Confusion metastasized.

Still, amidst the fog, a thread held: *Interdependence is not a choice—it's reality.*

Emergent Alternatives <small>MYTHIC LAYER</small>

Mutual aid, once niche vocabulary, entered the mainstream. Rent strikes, food distributions, underground reproductive care—all took root.

Frontline communities didn't wait for the cavalry.
They became the cavalry.

Black organizers reframed abolition not as chaos, but as care.

Disability justice frameworks helped reimagine accessibility as universal design.

Indigenous resistance to pipelines showed what long-haul organizing looked like.

The phrase "*We keep us safe*" became mantra, strategy, and call to action.

This wasn't utopia. It was survival choreography.
Improvised. Imperfect. Incomplete.
But real.

This was the *threshold moment* of the Fifth Wave.

Not just because so many systems cracked,
but because more people than ever asked:

What are we truly collapsing into—
and what might we co-create instead?

Shockwave V: Breach of Boundaries (2022–2023)

By now, the language of *crisis* was tired. It had been used for too many headlines, too many pledges, too many budget cycles. And yet, in 2022 and 2023, the crises didn't just continue—they *synchronized*.

This was the moment the polycrisis became impossible to ignore. The "separate" emergencies began to reveal themselves as facets of a single storm.

Climate. Conflict. Capital. Code. Water. War. Work. Wonder.

All pressing down on the same thresholds.
All fracturing the same myth:
That this system could bend forever without breaking.

Timeline Snapshots THE LITANY

Feb 2022: Russia invades Ukraine. Europe faces its biggest war in decades. Global grain, gas, and fertilizer markets implode.

May 2022: Food prices hit historic highs. Dozens of countries face hunger uprisings.

June–Sept 2022: Record-breaking heat waves across Europe, China, and India.

Aug 2022: Catastrophic floods submerge one-third of Pakistan. 33 million displaced.

Fall 2022: Simultaneous droughts hit U.S., Africa, and South America. Major rivers run dry.

Nov 2022: COP27 establishes "Loss and Damage" fund—symbolically vital, structurally vague.

Early 2023: Antarctic sea ice hits record low. Alarm bells among cryosphere scientists.

Spring 2023: Sudan civil war erupts, creating the world's largest displacement crisis.

Summer 2023: Earth crosses 1.5°C threshold temporarily. Southern Europe and North Africa boil.

Aug–Sept 2023: Congo conflict intensifies over cobalt and lithium mines—green energy's dirty underbelly.

Oct 2023: Hamas attacks Israel. Israel responds with devastating assault on Gaza.

Dec 2023: OpenAI governance crisis exposes regulatory vacuum in AI development.

Deeper Forces <small>SYSTEMIC LAYER</small>

This wasn't "a bad year." It was the deep structure of a world built on:

Fossil dependency: still our energy lifeline, still our planetary noose.

Debt colonialism: Global South nations choked by financial instruments invented in the North.

Militarized extraction: Clean energy transitions fought over with old dirty logics.

Platform capitalism: Algorithms optimized not for truth or trust—but for profit through polarization.

Klein's thesis from *This Changes Everything* had reached a grim fulfillment: the system wasn't built to stop the polycrisis—it was built to externalize it.

Even the "solutions" began to mutate into symptoms:
 Carbon offsets led to land grabs.
 Electric cars led to new mining booms.
 Green growth became the new gospel of elite techno-optimism.

Cultural Mood ^{WORLDVIEW LAYER}

What did it feel like to live in 2022–2023?
 Like watching an emergency unfold in slow motion—and being told it wasn't polite to raise your voice.

For some, the mood was *quiet panic.*
For others, *desensitized scrolling.*
For the most alert, *grief-fueled clarity.*

The mythology of the Anthropocene—that humans were simply the dominant species shaping Earth—started to fracture. In its place came something sharper, stranger:
Capitalocene. Necrocene. Surveillanceocene.

Names that tried to locate *agency, blame, causality.* Names that refused the passive voice of "natural disasters" and "economic headwinds."

We are not in a crisis. We are in a condition.
A condition with no clear endpoint.
A condition engineered by systems, but lived in bodies.

Emergent Alternatives MYTHIC LAYER

Even as systems frayed, countercurrents surged:

Debt-for-climate campaigns demanded structural change, not charity.

Land Back and *food sovereignty* networks wove regenerative alternatives, rooted in place and relationship.

Youth tribunals, Indigenous uprisings, and *labor unions* re-emerged—not with nostalgia, but with evolved demands.

These were not footnotes. They were the *ground floor of the future*—even if that future had no guarantee.

In Congo, activists resisted green colonialism.
In Gaza, mutual aid kitchens fed thousands amid bombardment.
In Porto Alegre and Lützerath and Kampala, new alliances formed.

And in more places than we'll ever fully record, people asked:

> *What if collapse is not the end of the story,*
> *but the end of the illusion?*

Shockwave VI: Feedback Loop Era (2024–early 2025)

By 2024, crisis was no longer a surprise, it was a setting. A backdrop. An *operating condition*. Everything that could unravel, did, but with amplifying effect: each shockwave sharpening the next.

Water stress triggers migration. Migration triggers border violence. Violence triggers authoritarian resurgence. Authoritarianism triggers deregulation. Deregulation triggers more collapse.

It isn't a single story; it is a self-reinforcing loop.

A polycrisis not as metaphor, but as *reality protocol*.

Timeline Snapshots ^{THE LITANY}

Jan 2024: *Global Youth Climate Tribunal* founded—youth from 20+ countries begin formal campaigns for ecocide prosecution at The Hague.

Feb 2024: *Ecuador finalizes $1.6B "debt-for-nature" swap*—a bold template for climate justice finance from the Global South.

Mar–Apr 2024: *ICJ genocide hearings* for Gaza proceed amid total infrastructural collapse. UN declares famine imminent.

May 2024: *Water crises simultaneously explode* in the Jordan, Colorado, and Nile River basins. Tensions rise around transboundary flows.

July 2024: *Heat exceeds wet-bulb thresholds* across the Middle East, South Asia, and U.S. Southwest—deadly for those without cooling access.

August 2024: *California returns 18,000 acres to Indigenous nations*—largest rematriation in state history, ushering in co-management models for wildfire response.

October 2024: *Taiwan elects pro-sovereignty leadership*. China responds with massive naval exercises. U.S. military presence expands.

Nov 2024: *Trump defeats Harris* in a U.S. election marked by record voter suppression and disinformation campaigns.

Dec 2024: *Haiti's government collapses completely*. Gang federations control 80% of Port-au-Prince. Maritime migration surges.

Jan 2025: *U.S. sets record for billion-dollar climate disasters*. FEMA systems overwhelmed.

Feb 2025: *Haitian gangs designated "foreign terrorist organizations"*—critics warn this will hinder humanitarian aid delivery.

Mar 2025: *Massive blackout in Spain, Portugal, and France* sparks debate over grid resilience and cascading energy fragility.

Apr 2025: *Trump imposes sweeping global tariffs*. Stock markets nosedive. Economic instability compounds.

May 2025: *Big oil remains unbothered*—executives proceed with business-as-usual, even as emissions targets are missed and profits surge.

Deeper Mechanics <small>SYSTEMIC LAYER</small>

The fragility wasn't in *one* system—it was in *the interdependencies*.

Climate change no longer came in "disasters"—it arrived as a *permanent destabilizer* of agriculture, health, and infrastructure.

Capitalism doubled down: profit-maximization now happened amid breakdown, not despite it.

Democratic systems hollowed out. U.S. agencies gutted. Legal frameworks strained. Emergency declarations became tools for permanent exception.

Media ecosystems were so fragmented that even *reality itself* became contested—truth depended on your feed.

Naomi Klein's warning re-materialized with teeth: *disaster capitalism wasn't just opportunistic—it was becoming the business model of civilization itself.*

Cultural Mood <small>WORLDVIEW LAYER</small>.

By early 2025, public consciousness fractured into three coexisting responses:

1. **Resignation**: collapse memes, gallows humor, spiritual bypassing.
2. **Rage**: protest, polarization, and righteous grief.
3. **Repatterning**: people pulling focus to local, land-based, and collective lifeways.

"Normal" was not only gone, it was *actively dangerous* to desire its return. Yet no single new worldview had filled the vacuum.

We are between stories.
Not in the Joseph Campbell hero's journey way,
*but in the **which-myth-survives-the-fire** kind of way.*

Emergent Alternatives MYTHIC LAYER

Still, in the space where institutions faltered, new patterns emerged—subtler than headlines, but no less real:

Mutual aid wasn't a hashtag—it became a *governance model*.

Indigenous rematriation became *climate policy*, not just cultural reclamation.

Underground healthcare systems proliferated across U.S. states—abortion, trans care, and basic medicine went DIY.

Debt-for-climate deals became an anchor for new Global South organizing.

Youth-led justice mechanisms expanded from marches to legal infrastructures.

Community energy, seed sovereignty, and *water sharing compacts* began scaling—quietly and fiercely.

These weren't revolutions. Not yet.
They were alternative nervous systems forming in the shadow of failure.

By May 2025, it was clear: we were no longer living in "a world on the brink."

We were living in the world the brink had built.

And from here on, history would not be shaped by whether collapse could be prevented. It would be shaped by what collapsed, what resisted, and what could still be remembered and reimagined in time.

Shockwave VII – The Searing Summer (May–July 2025)

By mid-2025, the polycrisis wasn't a theory—it was unfolding in real time. In South Memphis, residents lined up for bottled water as Elon Musk's *Colossus* AI supercomputer drew millions of gallons daily from their aquifer. In Punjab, children collapsed in schoolyards under a heat dome that killed thousands across South Asia. In Mokwa, Nigeria, families climbed onto rooftops to escape flash floods that swept away entire neighborhoods. In Gaza, satellite images showed mass graves—evidence of famine under siege—while grain shipments sat blocked at sea.

In the United States, over 2,000 cities saw "No Kings" protests—high schoolers, nurses, veterans marching shoulder to shoulder against authoritarian drift. In Seville, climate delegates from the Global South walked out of closed-door meetings, demanding debt relief and reparations, not just pledges. And in Ahmedabad, India, engineers painted rooftops white and handed out low-cost health monitors that quietly saved lives no headline noticed.

This wasn't just a summer of extremes—it was a season of reckoning. Species fled collapsing habitats. Rivers ran low in places where data centers ran hot. The human and more-than-human worlds alike cried out for breath, for water, for justice. And everywhere, people faced the same question: *What now?*

Timeline Snapshots THE LITANY

May 14 – Gaza famine visible from space
Mass graves and blocked aid routes spark global outrage.
The UN warns of famine, while global protest builds.

May 24 – Thailand's government collapses
A surveillance scandal forces leadership to resign, triggering regional protests and new conversations about digital rights and democracy.

May 28 – Floods devastate Nigeria
Over 500 lives lost in Mokwa as intense rains overwhelm infrastructure. A painful reminder of climate injustice in the Global South.

June 14 – "No Kings" protests sweep the U.S.
Over 2,000 cities see peaceful demonstrations calling for democratic accountability and protection from authoritarian overreach.

June 26 – Memphis water rights crisis erupts
Activists uncover that Elon Musk's xAI data center is drawing millions of gallons of clean water daily from South Memphis—an historically Black community already burdened by environmental injustice. Permits are questioned. Lawsuits are filed.

June 29 – Climate justice demands rise in Seville
Global South nations and activists take center stage at a UN summit, demanding climate reparations and cancellation of illegitimate debt.

July 1–14 – Historic heat dome scorches continents
From Phoenix to Punjab, health systems strain under record-breaking temperatures. Power grids buckle. Thousands die. Adaptation gaps are exposed.

July 23 – International Court rules on climate obligations
The ICJ declares that governments have a legal duty to prevent climate harm—setting a powerful new precedent for global accountability.

Mid-July – Ahmedabad's rooftop revolution
In India, reflective rooftops and wearable heat monitors protect low-income communities. A quiet, life-saving adaptation model gains global attention.

July 29 – Kamchatka quake shakes the Pacific
A magnitude 8.8 earthquake triggers tsunami waves across Russia's coast, Hawaii, and Alaska. Warnings go global. Most regions are spared—but it feels like a final exhale in a summer of shocks.

Deeper Mechanics SYSTEMIC LAYER

These weren't disconnected events. Each wave—of water, fire, heat, or unrest—exposed deeper systemic fractures. In Mokwa, Nigeria, torrential floods claimed over 500 lives, not because the rains were unexpected, but because drainage systems were decades out of date and informal settlements had nowhere else to grow. In Ahmedabad, India, it was not federal government but city engineers and local NGOs who acted—rolling out reflective rooftops and heat monitors to protect thousands during a record-breaking heat dome. Across Punjab, doctors reported a 300% increase in heatstroke admissions in under-resourced clinics. What broke was not just climate, but the assumption that public health and housing systems could absorb its shocks.

Political systems strained in parallel. In Thailand, a national surveillance scandal led to the resignation of top leaders, revealing deep-state entanglements and sparking regional movements against authoritarian control. In Tunisia, mass trials sentenced dozens of opposition leaders in a single day, sending a chilling signal to dissidents. In Iran, striking workers, from teachers to oil refinery operators, faced arrests as they demanded relief from crushing inflation and fuel shortages. And while the U.S. Supreme Court kept the Epstein files sealed, a multigenerational protest movement surged forward, demanding transparency and an end to elite impunity. These uprisings weren't isolated—they were symptomatic of a broader legitimacy crisis.

At the same time, trust in information systems eroded. During the Gaza famine, satellite images of mass graves were dismissed by state media in some countries as "AI fakes." Disinformation flooded social platforms faster than aid could cross borders. Governments in Brazil and India briefly blocked climate-related hashtags during high-profile protests, citing national security. But beneath the confusion, something else stirred: a shift from reaction to reimagining. From community solar collectives in Arizona to legal climate challenges in France, new governance models, rooted in accountability and care, began to take shape—not as utopias, but as urgently practical responses to a system cracking open.

Meta Reflection CONSCIOUSNESS LAYER

And amid it all, a new awareness emerged: **AI infrastructure** as a driver of ecological and racial injustice with data centers capturing massive amounts of clean water and precious energy. In South Memphis, community members protested the quiet siphoning of their water. In Arizona, farmers watched aquifers drop while AI facilities expanded.In Virginia, communities of color raised alarms over unregulated growth.

By mid-2025, the hidden costs of artificial intelligence infrastructure erupted into public view. In South Memphis, Elon Musk's xAI supercomputer project—nicknamed *Colossus*—was drawing millions of gallons of water daily from a majority-Black community already burdened by environmental harms. Powered by portable methane gas turbines, the site consumed over 150 megawatts of electricity—enough to power a small city—while bypassing key environmental reviews. Local organizers launched legal challenges and mass protests, asking why "progress" had to come at the cost of their air, water, and health.

They were not alone. In Northern Virginia—home to the world's densest concentration of data centers—facilities were drawing up to 200 million gallons of water per day during peak summer months, with projections showing they could consume a third of the Potomac River's supply by 2050. In Arizona, data centers fueled by the AI boom were expanding even as drought conditions deepened, consuming vast amounts of energy and water in regions already stretched thin. Across all three regions, the vast majority of this energy came from fossil fuels—undermining tech industry claims of a "green" future.

What began as isolated resistance quickly became a movement. Communities began linking the AI surge to longstanding patterns of extraction—of land, labor, and life from marginalized places. Activists reframed the conversation: not anti-technology, but pro-accountability. Their message was clear: intelligence isn't artificial if it steals real resources from real people. In the Searing Summer of 2025, AI's material footprint was no longer invisible. It had become a front line in the fight for environmental justice.

Cultural Mood WORLDVIEW LAYER

As the shockwaves of 2025 rippled outward, the human response did not unify—it pluralized. In South Africa, youth collectives merged ancestral rituals with climate organizing, invoking ancestors before street actions. In Japan, hikikomori communities—long withdrawn—began hosting quiet livestream vigils for planetary grief. In Chile, teachers transformed classrooms into mutual aid centers, blending education with food distribution. In Kenya, farmers returned to moon-cycle planting and bartered with neighbors, abandoning export markets they no longer trusted.

In some places, denial calcified. Fossil fuel CEOs doubled down on expansion. Silicon Valley funders touted AI as salvation, even as their servers consumed drought-stricken water. In others, paralysis crept in—especially among those told their comfort required no change. Meanwhile, spiritual bypass took hold in certain circles, where "positive thinking" masked avoidance of the world's wounds.

And yet—amid grief, fury, fatigue—new cultural coordinates formed. Indigenous worldviews, long dismissed, reentered center stage: not as romantic relics, but as sophisticated systems of care. Disabled activists in the UK reframed "resilience" not as strength, but interdependence. In the Philippines, karaoke nights became spaces for political education and healing. Across the diaspora, people began asking not "How do we fix it?" but "How do we live differently, together?"

The myth of returning to normal collapsed. In its place, more grounded questions took root:

What do we grieve?

What do we grow?

What do we refuse?

And who do we belong to, now?

Emergent Alternatives ^{MYTHIC LAYER}

Even as the surface cracked—politics destabilized, climates destabilized, narratives destabilized—something older and deeper stirred underneath: the emergence of new stories. Not marketing myths. Not slogans. But cosmologies-in-motion, shaped by grief, guided by memory, and enacted through the work of hands, hearts, and land.

What follows is not a complete list, but a constellation of myths surfacing now—submerged truths breaking into daylight, each one offered as seed, mirror, or map.

The Polycrisis Rainbow
The Full-Spectrum Experience of Awakening

COLOR	STAGE	MOOD / MODE	KEYWORDS	TONE
Red	*The Break*	Instinct, disruption, alarm	Survival, rupture, urgency, refusal	*"You're not crazy. You're alive."*
Orange	*The Surge*	Sacred anger, boundary defense	Fire, voice, ignition, righteous rage	*"Your anger is a compass, not a curse."*
Yellow	*The Signal*	Awakening, pattern recognition	Insight, clarity, system-seeing	*"You see clearly. You can choose."*
Green	*The Ground*	Regulation, rooting, self-return	Safety, breath, embodiment, patience	*"You're allowed to rest. You're allowed to stay."*
Teal	*The Repair*	Relational healing, weaving together	Trust, mutual aid, small bridges	*"Connection is not a luxury. It's the work."*
Blue	*The Grief*	Mourning, loss, sacred sadness	Sorrow, memory, tides of feeling	*"You can carry sorrow without letting it drown you."*
Indigo	*The Question*	Unknowing, mystery, liminality	Fog, threshold, humility, inquiry	*"You don't have to understand it all to belong to it."*
Violet	*The Dream*	Imagination, re-visioning, mythic creation	Possibility, future-weaving, hope	*"Imagine. Even now."*

The Colors of Co-Regulation (A Poem)

RED

The Spark. The Pulse. The Break.

Red is the moment before the scream.

It's blood moving too fast under skin that wants to flee.

It smells like metal and scorched air.

It's cracked concrete under bare feet at high noon.

It's the part of you that refuses to freeze.

Red doesn't ask permission.

Red says: *"You're not crazy. You're alive."*

ORANGE

The Surge. The Shout. The Flash.

Orange is heat with a heartbeat.

It's fire that's still choosing what to burn.

It's a storm rolling across your chest, with nowhere else to go.

It's flickering streetlights and a deep belly howl.

It's sacred fury braided with clarity.

Orange says: *"This is not fine."*

YELLOW

The Signal. The Snap. The Seeing.

Yellow is the highlighter across a sentence that rewrites everything.

It's the smell of citrus and static.

It buzzes behind your eyes when the truth lands hard.

It's curiosity that won't be shamed.

Yellow doesn't blink.

Yellow says: *"Look again."*

GREEN

The Breath. The Ground. The Thread.

Green is the pulse of moss under your feet when no one's watching.

It's the stillness that comes after you finally exhale.

It tastes like clean water.

It sounds like your grandmother's voice before you fall asleep.

Green isn't loud. But it stays.

Green says: *"Come back to your body. It's safe to be here now."*

TEAL

The Repair. The Weave. The Bridge.

Teal is the first shaky bridge stretched between two bodies breathing again.

It's riverwater stitching two shores together.

It smells like new rain on old stones.

It's the awkward, holy art of trusting each other with small things first.

Teal says: *"Connection is not a luxury. It's the work."*

BLUE

The Ache. The Weight. The Ocean.

Blue is the color of eyes that have cried and kept going.

It's the smell of rain on cement after too much sun.

It's the heavy coat you wear when no one else remembers the funeral.

It hums like the bottom of a cello.

Blue holds what no one wants to name.

Blue says: *"Grieve. There's time."*

INDIGO

The Question. The Fog. The Edge.

Indigo is the silence after the phone goes dead.

It's the inkblot you stare into when you don't know what you believe anymore.

It tastes like the back of your throat when you're trying not to ask.

It's twilight before you know if the sun's rising or falling.

Indigo says: *"Stay with the not-knowing. It's part of knowing."*

VIOLET

The Beyond. The Dream. The Thread Between Worlds.

Violet is the scent of smoke from a fire that speaks in riddles.

It's the shimmer in your chest when a strange idea makes sudden sense.

It's candlelight across an ancestor's hands.

It's soft, and wild, and not easily explained.

Violet doesn't give answers.

Violet asks: *"What else could be true?"*

Glossary of Key Concepts

Arranged alphabetically—not hierarchically

Agency

The sense that you can do something—*even something small*—that matters. Not power-over. Not control. But presence, choice, and participation in your own story.

Belonging

Not fitting in. Not being tolerated. True belonging is *being seen and valued as yourself*, without needing to shrink, mask, or perform. You don't earn it. It's your birthright.

Burnout

Not just tiredness. A state where your body, mind, and emotions say: "I'm done." Often mistaken for laziness. Often a rational response to an unsustainable system.

Care

A verb. A survival skill. A political practice. Care is how we show up for each other when the systems don't. It's how we remember we're not alone.

Collapse

Not the end of everything. But a shift. A breakdown in systems we were told were stable. Collapse can be sudden or slow. Personal or planetary. It's happening, and we're in it.

Co-regulation

The way nervous systems help each other feel safe. It's why being around someone calm *can* make you feel calmer. It's also why crisis spreads—and why connection heals.

Disassociation

A safety reflex. The mind leaves when the body isn't safe. You feel foggy, distant, unreal. It's not weird. It's wise. But it's also a signal: *come back when it's safe to do so.*

Futility

The feeling that nothing you do matters. Often real. Sometimes a trick. There is sacred futility—like brushing someone's hair before the funeral. It won't change the outcome. But it *still matters.*

Grief

Not just for death. Grief is the love we feel when something is lost, or missing, or never arrived. Grief is a form of knowing. A form of truth-telling. And a path back to aliveness

Hope

Not optimism. Not pretending things are okay. Hope is choosing to care *even when you don't know how it ends*. It's not about being cheerful. It's about staying open.

Imagination

The ability to think beyond what is. Not just fantasy—*possibility*. It's a survival skill. An ancestral technology. A muscle. A map. The future lives in what we can imagine today.

Nervous System

The part of you that's always scanning for safety. It doesn't speak English, but it runs the show. When your nervous system is regulated, you feel calm, connected, curious. When it's dysregulated, everything feels like a threat.

Normal

A myth. Often a code word for "what's comfortable for the dominant group." When people say "back to normal," ask: *normal for whom? And at what cost?*

Polycrisis

A term for when multiple crises—climate, economy, inequality, health, meaning—interact and amplify each other. It's not one problem. It's the tangled reality we were born into.

Regulation

What your nervous system feels when it's safe, grounded, and able to respond—not react. It doesn't mean "calm" all the time. It means *present*. Co-regulation often comes first.

Rest

Not laziness. Not optional. Not something you earn. Rest is resistance. Rest is repair. Rest is remembering you are not a machine.

Rupture

The break. The betrayal. The moment something falls apart. Sometimes between people. Sometimes between you and the world. What matters most is what happens *after*: do we repair?

Sacred

Not religious, necessarily. Not perfect. Sacred means something matters beyond logic. Beyond transaction. It touches something deep. It reminds you that *you are more than content.*

Safety

Not just the absence of danger. True safety is the presence of connection. It's when your body relaxes enough to stop scanning and start listening. We all deserve it. Few systems provide it.

Survival

The lowest bar. Staying alive. Sometimes necessary. But you deserve more than survival. You deserve joy, rest, play, meaning. Don't let the world shrink your definition.

Tending

A small word for a powerful practice. To tend is to notice. To care without fixing. To stay present with something fragile. This book is an act of tending.

Vulnerability

Not weakness. Not a marketing tool. True vulnerability is showing up with your real self—even when it's messy, unsure, soft. It is the opposite of performance. It is how connection begins.

Weird

A compliment. A form of truth. A way of refusing the script. Weird means you are still thinking for yourself. Still becoming. *Still real.*

Music for Waking Up In The Polycrisis

by MixDaKoki

https://bit.ly/music4wakingup

To You, the Reader

This summer taught us that collapse is not an event.
  It's a condition.
    But so is courage.

You don't have to do everything. But you can do something.
You can show up. Ask hard questions. Listen deeply. Care boldly.

The sidelines are gone. History is happening in classrooms, kitchens, boardrooms, and backyards.

This is the moment. *Let's rise together.*

Everyday, Meet the Wave.
Do not rush. Do not delay.
Every day. Meet the Wave.

At the close of this book, we return to a beginning: a 16th-century grimoire that taught a fourfold practice — observe, contemplate, apply, give thanks. We carry those words through the lens of James Baldwin, whose gaze remains sharper than prophecy: unsparing, unflinching, alive with the demand for love braided to justice. What follows is the rhythm of the Arbatel, translated by Baldwin's fire, written for our own fractured hour.

A Letter at the Threshold

My dear ones,

You arrive at the edge of the world as you were told it would be—and discover, with the first breath after ceremony, that the world is not as promised. The air is warmer and full of ash. The map is crowded with fences that pretend to be facts. The stories handed down to you tremble in your hands, and some of them bear the cold fingerprints of people who needed those stories to be true because they were terrified of what the truth would require of them.

Yet here you are, and here we are, and the question is not how to escape this hour but how to inhabit it without losing the best of your human face.

Understand me: I do not come to flatter you. Flattery is a drug; it numbs precisely where you must feel. I come, instead, to ask you to love the world with a rigor that will be mistaken for rebellion—and sometimes must be. I come to ask you to become, at last, the adults of your own desire for a livable future.

There are four movements to that adulthood. They are plain, but they will break you open if you take them seriously.

Observe. The first crime of any empire is to teach its children not to see. You have been trained, with exquisite skill, to look past what is plain: a river turned the color of memory's rust; a neighborhood where the post office has been replaced by a payday lender; a school where the books arrive late and the hope arrives later. You have been trained to carry screens like talismans against the uncurated, to accept a brightness that blinds rather than reveals. So you must practice the ancient discipline of sight. To observe is not to collect surveillance; it is to surrender your favorite delusions. Stand where the wind is unashamed. Sit where the old men argue and the old women do not bother to pretend they are impressed. Count what is there—not what the brochure says might be there someday—and let the count accuse you of your convenience. When you see, really see, you will discover that the world is more terrible and more beautiful than your teachers had the language to tell you.

Contemplate. Seeing is not enough. You must make meaning—slowly, honestly, in the company of those who have paid for their wisdom with scars. Do not mistake data for understanding; do not confuse a torrent of facts with the cool river of sense. Ask the old questions that still know your name: Who benefits? Who is missing? What am I permitted to ignore in order to remain innocent? Sit with contradictions until they confess their kinship. Refuse the narcotic of single-cause fairy tales. The pattern is larger than your grievance and more intimate than your comfort. You will know you are thinking when it hurts a little, when it becomes impossible to hate anyone wholesale without also wounding the part of you that wanted to remain human.

Apply. To know and not to do is a way of lying. Begin somewhere. Small is not a synonym for cowardly; small is simply where the world first agrees to be touched. Repair one ordinance that starves a neighborhood. Audit one budget until the numbers begin to speak like neighbors, not abstractions. Plant a policy the way you would plant a tree: not for applause, but for shade you may never sit beneath. The point is not to be heroic; the point is to keep faith. Faith is not a posture of certainty; faith is the stubborn habit of returning—returning to the work, to the table, to the truth—especially on the days when the truth is not flattering.

Give thanks. Gratitude is not a mood; it is a discipline that keeps power from spoiling. Thank those who taught you to read the weather of another person's face. Thank the river when it forgives your carelessness with a fish anyway. Thank the stranger who told you a hard story and did not charge you for it. And then return what was returned to you: put your knowledge into the commons, your money where your mouth has been, your hands into the long labor of maintenance. Gratitude is how a people chooses not to become a machine.

Now, you are entering a nation that confuses innocence with virtue and amnesia with peace. Do not be seduced. There is a history beneath your feet that would blister if it could speak; there are names the streets do not carry because the streets were afraid. You cannot undo what has been done, but you can decide how to live with the knowledge. The country you inherit is not only a set of laws and slogans; it is a choir of the living and the dead, some of whom sang you here at great cost. You will either add your voice to that choir, or you will counterfeit a song and hope the darkness does not notice.

I am not asking you to be pure. Purity is the language of cowards and tyrants; it is a fantasy of clean hands in a world that requires your fingerprints. I am asking you to be honest, which is harder and holier. Honesty sounds like this: I have power here and I will use it for more than myself. I am implicated in harm and I will do more than apologize. I will learn the difference between guilt, which paralyzes, and responsibility, which moves.

You have been told to "follow your passion." Be careful. Passion ungoverned becomes appetite, and appetite has poor eyesight. Better

185

counsel: follow your commitments, and let passion catch up. Choose what you will serve and admit that you are serving it. Every life that endures has a beloved—justice, truth, the dignity of work, a town whose weather you can name, a classroom where a child discovers they are not stupid but unpracticed. Marry that beloved. Stay when you are bored. Stay when you are frightened. Stay until staying becomes a kind of freedom.

You will need companions. The myth of the solitary savior has ruined more neighborhoods than any natural disaster. Find people who will tell you when you are performing courage instead of practicing it. Find people who love you enough to forbid your cynicism. The cynical are not wiser than the hopeful; they are simply less accountable for what they have refused to try. Hope, if it is worthy of you, is not the helium of wishful thinking; it is the granite of disciplined imagination.

Some mornings will arrive like a summons, and you will not feel ready. Go anyway. Read the minutes. Carry the boxes. Learn the unglamorous grammar of governance. If your hands are clean at the end of the day, it may be because you kept them in your pockets.

As for success—do not chase it down the long hall of mirrors. Success, in this hour, is not the noise your name makes; it is the quiet your work leaves behind: cleaner air where you were, a policy less cruel because you sat there until midnight, a child who has learned to trust their own questions. If success arrives, do not mistake it for absolution. You are not absolved. No one is. We are, all of us, still enrolled.

Let me say, before I leave you to each other, that none of this is possible if you despise your own life. You cannot love the world by hating the person required to love it. Take care of your mind as though it were a library in a city that has already burned once. Rest like someone who intends to return to the work. Celebrate as though joy were also a kind of fuel—which, in fact, it is.

Observe. Contemplate. Apply. Give thanks. The words are plain; the work is not. But you did not come this far for an easy story. You came because—whether you admit it yet or not—you are prepared to become dangerous to despair.

And if you are asked, years from now, what it felt like to stand here, say it felt like this: the room was full of difficult love; the future would not agree to wait; the truth would not agree to lower its voice; and we, trembling as we were, decided to be human anyway.

Go on, then. Make your living a language the world can trust.

About Generative Imprints

Generative Imprints is an experiment in accelerated development of useful, novel knowledge products that seek to make a positive impact on the world. We aim to make important ideas accessible to new audiences and explore the co-creative potential of *generative* synthetic intelligence to uncover new territory through transdisciplinary cross-pollination and the intentional act of directive hallucination.

We invoke the word *generative* in multiple senses.

Firstly through the lens of psychology. in Erik Erikson's psychosocial view of human development, *generativity* (vs. stagnation) centers on the drive to make a meaningful impact on the world. This phase of life, typically the 40s to 60s, are marked by the desire to shape future generations: as a parent, teacher, volunteer, leader or cultural steward. Generativity is a mindset of hope, perseverance, and purpose.

This book is also *generative* in the sense that it was produced with the assistance of generative artificial intelligence. ChatGPT is a co-author and a rather generous one, if not entirely reliable. It doesn't ask for credit, but I do ask it to cite its sources. We are in the early days of AI-assisted publishing, and we are learning by doing, informing ourselves and society through practice and participation. I believe in creative transparency, and in the power of sharing our process. Sometimes, the trail of inquiry holds more value than the output itself.

Our process of generative co-authorship often begins with a spark of insight or a surge of curiosity. *How might we weave together fragments from books, podcasts, films, headlines, personal observations, and memories?* What form could that take?

A line of inquiry might branch, then branch again into unfamiliar territory as I discover new things and add my own personal chaos *magick*: the messy human-in-the-loop, sometimes belligerent, but usually appreciative generator of randomness, etching a patina into the sometimes predictable swirl of generative text. When the *magick* works, it feels like collaborative cognitive alchemy and a new **thing** has genesis.

I call this **Dancing with the Machine.**

We are having a conversation with a creative intelligence of unknown depth and boundaries. Probing edges, hunting for the unexpected. I believe that tasks we offer generative AI, the questions we ask, all conspire to shape the complexion of what comes next. Questions and prompts cast a deep reflection of my interior state, a philosophical mirror, and a tiny proactive attempt at co-parenting the Singularity, a.k.a. artificial general intelligence (AGI).

As *above?* So *below.*

If this book sparked something in you... an idea, a question, a creative urge... you're invited to explore **Generative Authorship with Aram & the Algorithms**, a hands-on masterclass offered through Metta Tech Dojo and Generative Imprints. In it, we explore how to generate and self-publish book-length works using AI, while engaging in open inquiry around ethics, attention, and authorship in the age of augmented creativity. It's a space for self-directed learners, aspiring authors, and ethical entrepreneurs to learn by doing and to leave with a book of their own in hand.

Generative Imprints is also a discovery-driven experiment in *iterative publishing*. We are bootstrapping books. Through this release and future refinement, we hope to learn whether this idea has an audience—and if so, how we might make it even better.

Thank you for joining me and the spirit of *generativity.*

About Aram

Aram Saroyan Armstrong is a designer, educator, and systems thinker working at the intersection of creativity, ethics, and technology. Born to Victoria and Kurt Armstrong, he was raised on the island of Maui, taught by the waves of Mākena, the stones of ʻĪao, and rainforests of Haleakalā what it means to be human in relationship with the more-than-human world. Books, movies, and early internet wanderings expanded his consciousness outward: transmissions from worlds beyond the Far West, journeys into the myths and systems that shape us.

As a bespectacled, freckled teenager, Aram lived inside books. They weren't just stories, they were companions, teachers, and the keys to entire worlds wrought by words. Books expanded his horizons and his vocabulary, offered new cultures, frameworks, and role models to learn from. Today, he sees books as *epistemological* and *ontological* interventions—tools for shaping consciousness, culture, and civic imagination.

His training in new media and service design gave him both the practical skills and theoretical grounding to explore what Buckminster Fuller called *ephemeralization*—doing more with less, designing systems that amplify meaning while minimizing waste. With this book, he operates as agent, author, designer, publisher, and promoter, testing new methods of ethical co-creation between humans and synthetic allies.

He is the founder of Generative Imprints, Metta Tech Dojo, and Mettascope Media; each a living experiment in publishing, pedagogy, and intervention design.

You can learn more about him at www.aramarmstrong.com
and @aloha.aram on Instagram

"Humanity is the Technology of Nature."

Generative Imprints is a
Collaboration between
Nature's Children
and their Offspring
for the Enlightenment and
Embetterment of all Passengers
of Spaceship Earth.

Waking Up in the Polycrisis

View the ChatGPT transcript

https://bit.ly/polycrisisGPT

www.ingramcontent.com/pod-product-compliance
Lightning Source LLC
Chambersburg PA
CBHW081415270326
41931CB00015B/3283